Contents

Questions Kids Ask About the Bible

Questions Kids Ask About Life

Quick Children's Sermons 2: Why Did God Make Mosquitoes?

Group

Loveland, Colorado

Quick Children's Sermons 2:
Why Did God Make Mosquitoes?

CREDITS
Contributing Authors: Robin Christy, Nanette Goings, Amy Nappa, Lori Haynes Niles, Helen Turnbull, Beth Rowland Wolf, and Carol Smith
Acquisitions Editor: Jody Brolsma
Editor: Jan Kershner
Creative Book Development Editor: David Thornton
Chief Creative Officer: Joani Schultz
Copy Editor: Pamela Shoup
Art Director: Kari K. Monson
Designer: Jean Bruns
Cover Art Director: Jeff A. Storm
Computer Graphic Artist: Rosalie Lawrence
Cover Illustrator: Stacey Lamb
Production Manager: Peggy Naylor

Unless otherwise noted, Scripture taken from the HOLY BIBLE, NEW INTERNATIONAL VERSION®. Copyright © 1973, 1978, 1984 by International Bible Society. Used by permission of Zondervan Publishing House. All rights reserved.

Library of Congress Cataloging-in-Publication Data
Quick children's sermons 2 : why did God make mosquitoes?
     p.   cm.
   Includes indexes.
   ISBN 0-7644-2052-6 (alk. paper)
   1. Children's sermons.
BV4315.Q54 1998
252'.53--dc21   97-49573
                                                  CIP

10 9 8 7 6 5 4 3 2 1   07 06 05 04 03 02 01 00 99 98
Printed in the United States of America.

Introduction

What does God do for fun?
Did Jesus ever spill his milk?
What will my room look like in heaven?

Have you ever been stumped by a big question from a little child? If so, this book is for you!

Quick Children's Sermons 2: Why Did God Make Mosquitoes? is a must for anyone who strives to engage and encourage children in their love for God. Instead of talking down to kids, the sermons in this book meet kids on their level, and introduce biblical truths in a format that will fascinate your little flock.

Each quick sermon is based on Scripture and answers a biblical question in a simple way kids will understand and enjoy. And since each message is active and fun, kids won't fidget and forget the important truth conveyed. Plus, with the handy "Simple Supplies" section, anyone can present a meaningful message with little preparation and even less anxiety.

But don't be fooled into thinking that the questions answered here are merely childish musings. After all, what adult hasn't wondered what God looks like or how God can be everywhere at one time? While the messages are perfect for kids during Sunday morning worship, children's church, Sunday school, or club programs, adults will be drawn into deeper reflection of God and his workings.

In the short time that *Quick Children's Sermons: Will My Dog Be in Heaven?* has been out, we've had so many requests for more that we're proud to present this new collection of quick, active-learning children's sermons.

We know you've been waiting for more, so enjoy these all-new, all-fun sermons! (And, oh yes—turn to page 85 for ideas on why God really did make mosquitoes!)

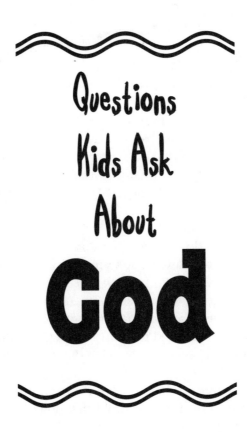

Questions Kids Ask About God

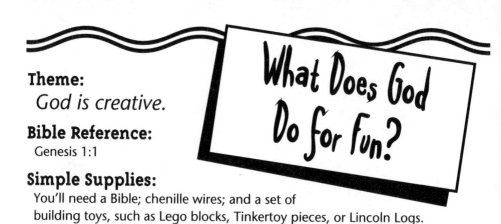

Theme:
God is creative.

Bible Reference:
Genesis 1:1

Simple Supplies:
You'll need a Bible; chenille wires; and a set of building toys, such as Lego blocks, Tinkertoy pieces, or Lincoln Logs.

For a lot of people, Sunday afternoon is a time to do fun stuff. Some people read the comics from the Sunday paper. Some people watch football games on television. Some people take naps, and they look forward to their Sunday afternoon nap all week long.

Do you have plans for this afternoon? Tell me about them. *Allow the children to respond.*

Have you ever wondered what God does? Sometimes I wonder about that. We all know that God can do anything, but sometimes I wonder what God plans to do on any particular day. There's something else I wonder about, too. What do you suppose God does for fun? *Allow the children to respond.*

Those are all wonderful, creative ideas. The Bible doesn't tell us very much about what God does from day to day. But the Bible does tell us about some of the marvelous things God has done. In fact, the Bible begins by telling us about something amazing that God did. *Open your Bible to Genesis 1:1, and show children the verse.*

The very first verse in the Bible says, "In the beginning God created the heavens and the earth." I bet that was fun! What do you think it might have been like to make the mountains or the stars? Which part of heaven or earth do you think would have been the most fun to make?

I brought something with me today to help us understand that first verse in the Bible. *Show the children the building toy you've brought.* Let's spend a few minutes creating. Let's pass the pieces out, and then we'll take turns adding them all together to make one big creation. *Pass out the pieces, and guide the children in putting their pieces together to form some sort of creation—a tower, a wall, or a building.*

What is this thing we've created? Do you enjoy building things? How do you think God feels when he creates new and beautiful things? *Allow the children to respond as you ask each question.*

Everything we see around us was created by God—even the things that we build ourselves were first created by God, because God made the building materials. Out of all the things God created, what's your favorite?

8

I think God had lots of fun creating our world. Let's thank God for his creation. I'll say, "Thank you, God, for..." and we'll go around our group. Each of you will have a chance to thank God for something. Ready? Here we go. ❤ "Thank you, God, for..." *Go around the group, and have each child finish the sentence. Then have kids offer a group* "Amen." ❤

Now I have something special to give you that will help you remember God's creation. *Bring out the chenille wires, and give one to each child.* Take this chenille wire back to your seat, and bend it into some kind of new creation. While you're creating, think about how much fun God had when he created the world.

Theme:
Wherever we worship, God is with us.

Does God Ever Skip Church?

Bible Reference:
Matthew 18:20

Simple Supplies:
You'll need a Bible and transparent tape.

Who knows what the word impossible means? *Let kids answer.*
The word impossible means that something can't be done. Let's try some impossible things. First, raise your fingers up in the air, but leave your hands in your lap. Can you do it? I didn't think so. It's impossible.

Now sit perfectly straight with your head facing the congregation. Without turning your head at all, look over to the wall on your right with one eye. At the same time, with your other eye, look over at the wall on your left. Can you do it? I didn't think so. It's impossible. What else can you think of that's impossible?

Now I'm going to ask you a question about God. You tell me if you think it's possible or impossible. Is it possible for God to skip church? *Allow children to respond.* I think that's a pretty tough question. We know that God can do anything, so it seems that if God wanted to skip church he could do it. But we also know that God loves worship, and he always keeps his promises.

There's a promise in the Bible about God and worship. *Open your Bible to Matthew 18:20, and show children the verse.* In Matthew 18:20, Jesus says, "For where two or three come together in my name, there am I with them."

We already found out that every time you lift your fingers, your hands are lifted too. And we found out that if your right eye looks towards something, your left eye looks toward the same thing. It's also true that every time we worship God together, God is right there with us. God never skips church. He's always here with us. Let's thank God.

♥ God, we love to worship you because you are wonderful. Thank you for promising to always be with us when we worship. We know that no matter where we are, you've promised to stay with us. Amen. ♥

To help us remember that God is with us when we worship, I'll put a piece of tape on the back of your hand to remind you that God sticks with us and is always with us when we worship him. *Put short pieces of tape on the backs of children's hands.*

What's God's Favorite Song?

Theme:
*God likes it when
we praise him.*

Bible Reference:
Psalm 150

Simple Supplies:
You'll need a Bible, jingle bells with curling ribbon securely tied on, a tape recorder, and cassettes with different kinds of praise music (a hymn, a contemporary praise song, and a children's praise song that kids know).

Do you think God has a favorite song? What do you think it is? Why? *Allow children to respond to each of your questions.*
Today I brought a tape recorder to help us think about what music God might enjoy. Let's listen to some different kinds of music. As you listen, think about how God might feel when he hears this music of praise to him. *Play a brief portion of each song.*

How do you think God feels when he hears music? *Allow children to respond.* Now I want you to vote on which song you think God likes best. Raise your hand if you think God likes the hymn best. Let me play it for you briefly to refresh your memory. *Play the hymn again for a few seconds.* If you voted for this song, why do you think this music is God's favorite?

Now raise your hand if you think God likes the praise song best. *Play that song for a few seconds.* Why do you think God likes that song?

Finally, raise your hand if you think God likes the children's praise song best. *Play that song briefly.* Why do you think God likes that song best?

Raise your hand if you think God likes all of these songs! Why do you think God likes them all?

Hold up your Bible. In Psalm 150, the Bible tells us about the kind of praise music God enjoys. Listen to this. "Praise the Lord. Praise God in his sanctuary; praise him in his mighty heavens. Praise him for his acts of power; praise him for his surpassing greatness. Praise him with the sounding of the trumpet, praise him with the harp and lyre, praise him with tambourine and dancing, praise him with the strings and flute, praise him with the clash of cymbals, praise him with resounding cymbals. Let everything that has breath praise the Lord. Praise the Lord."

What does that tell you about the kind of music God likes? How wonderful that God just loves to hear us praise him! He enjoys our praise with instruments, with singing, and with dancing. We don't have to sing just one kind of song, because God enjoys all the different sounds and songs of praise that are raised up to him.

Let's do some praising right now! Here's a bell for each of you. *Give each child one of the bells with the curling ribbons.* Shake your bell or clap and sing along with this praise song. *Play the children's praise song, and invite the children and congregation to sing along.*

That was wonderful! What do you think God is feeling as he hears our voices of praise? Isn't is great that we can do something that gives God pleasure?

Right now, let's use our voices to pray to God. ❤ Dear God, thank you for enjoying our praise. Help us to remember to praise you every day. We love you! In Jesus' name, amen. ❤

Take your bell home as a reminder that God's favorite song is any song that we sing in praise to him. He loves to hear our praises, so use your bell and your voice to praise him often!

Theme:

Our tithes and offerings help those in need.

Bible Reference:

Deuteronomy 15:10-11

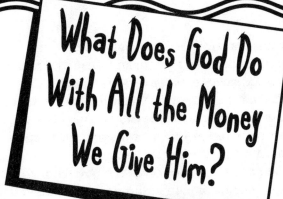

Simple Supplies:

You'll need a Bible; a large cardboard box;
crayons and markers; transparent tape; and pictures
of a family, a broken-down car, a snowstorm, and a sick person or doctor's office.
In advance, find out what kinds of donations are most needed in your community
by asking a local relief agency, such as a food bank, rescue mission, or shelter.

Did you know that every week people give money to the church?
Maybe you give money to God too. God uses the leaders of the
church to spend the money wisely so we can meet the needs of the
body of Christ. The body of Christ means us, the church.

What do you think the church leaders do with the money? How do you
think they spend the money? How much money do you think it costs to
run our church for one month? What part of running the church do you
think costs the most? *Allow the children to respond.*

The money is used to pay the pastor who teaches us about God. It's used
to help support missionaries, or people who tell others about Jesus. The
money is also used to heat the building and keep the lights on and the water
running. The church leaders buy the supplies to keep the building clean,
along with supplies to teach all of the Sunday school classes.

But inside the church isn't the only place the money is used. It's also
used for people outside the church. The book of Deuteronomy tells us more
about helping others.

Open your Bible to Deuteronomy 15:10-11. Listen to what the Bible says.
"Give generously to [your needy brother] and do so without a grudging
heart; then because of this the Lord your God will bless you in all your work
and in everything you put your hand to. There will always be poor people in
the land. Therefore I command you to be openhanded toward your brothers
and toward the poor and needy in your land."

According to the Bible, how else does God want us to use our money?
That's right! God wants us to use the money to help people in need.

Hold up the picture of the family, then pass the picture around. Let's pretend that this is a family in our neighborhood, and the husband just lost his job. Then their car breaks down, and there's no money to get it fixed. *Pass around the picture of the broken-down car.*

Next, a snowstorm hits, and the family can't pay to heat the house. *Pass around the picture of the snowstorm.* Then, because it's so cold, they get sick and can't afford medicine or to go to the doctor's office. *Pass around the picture of a sick person or doctor's office.*

Sometimes people don't even have enough money to live in a house or an apartment. Sometimes those people have to live in their car or even on the street. People in situations like that would be called homeless.

How would you feel if your family didn't have enough money for food or for a place to live? Wouldn't it be nice to have someone help you? It's God's desire that his church would be a place where people can go to get that help.

Collect the pictures, and set the box with the crayons, markers, and tape inside it in front of the children. For the next few weeks, let's fill this box with items to help needy people in our community. I called a local agency, and they gave me a list of items that people need the most.

As I read this list, you might hear of something that you know you have at home that you can bring next week. *Turn to the congregation.* To all the dads and moms and brothers and sisters in Christ, would you partner with us in filling this box? Maybe you could commit to bringing something on this list too. *Read the list of needed items to the children and the congregation.*

Right now, let's decorate this box to show that we want to obey God by helping the needy. Then we'll put the box in the lobby so it's ready for donations! I can't wait until this box is full and we can take it to (the designated charity organization).

Let kids tape the pictures to the box and decorate it with markers and crayons. Now let's close our time with a prayer together.

❤ Dear God, thank you for your Word that tells us to help those in need. Please help us to be generous and ready to share. We want to show our love for you by loving others. Amen. ❤

Theme:
We can give God gifts every day.

Bible Reference:
Matthew 25:34-40

Simple Supplies:
You'll need a Bible and three paper bags with a bow stuck on each one. In the first bag, place a few food items and a water bottle. In the second bag, place a few articles of clothing. In the third bag, place a heart sticker for each child.

L ook at these fun gift bags I brought as gifts to God. What do you think is inside these bags? What do you think would be a gift God would appreciate?

Open your Bible to Matthew 25:34-40, and show children the passage. In the book of Matthew, Jesus tells us a wonderful story about how to show kindness to others. As I tell the story, I'll do some actions, and I want you to follow me by doing the same actions. Ready?

The story begins with a group of people standing before a king. "Then the King will say to those on his right, 'Come, you who are blessed by my Father; take your inheritance, the kingdom prepared for you since the creation of the world. For I was hungry and you gave me something to eat *(rub your stomach)*, I was thirsty and you gave me something to drink *(act out drinking water)*, I was a stranger and you invited me in *(motion with your hand to invite someone over)*, I needed clothes and you clothed me *(rub your clothes like you're wearing something new)*, I was sick and you looked after me *(pretend to cough and sneeze)*, I was in prison and you came to visit me.' *(Shake hands with someone.)*

"Then the righteous will answer him, 'Lord, when did we see you hungry and feed you *(rub your stomach)*, or thirsty and give you something to drink? *(Act out drinking water.)* When did we see you a stranger and invite you in *(motion with your hand to invite someone over)*, or needing clothes and clothe you? *(Rub your clothes like you're wearing something new.)* When did we see you sick or in prison and go to visit you?' *(Shake hands with someone.)*

"The King will reply, 'I tell you the truth, whatever you did for one of the least of these brothers of mine, you did for me.' "

This means that if we treat people with kindness, we're actually giving a gift to God. Isn't that wonderful to know? If we want to show God that we love him, we need to show love to others.

Let's take a look inside these bags for clues about how we can be kind to others. I need a few children to open this first bag. *Choose several children to help you open the first bag.* Open the bag and show us what's inside. *Have your helpers remove the food and water and hold the items up for all to see.* How could we use this food and this water to show kindness to others? *Allow children to respond, and offer a few suggestions if they seem stumped.*

Now I need a few children to open this second bag. *Choose several other children to help open the next bag.* Open the bag and show us what's inside. *Have your helpers take out the clothes and hold them up for all to see.* How could we use these clothes to show kindness to others? *Allow children to respond.*

Those are all great ideas! You really know how to help others! And you know what else? Food, water, and clothes aren't the only ways to help those in need. We can show love and kindness right in our own homes, with our families. And we can show love and kindness at school, and even at church!

What are some ways to show love and kindness to others at home? *Kids might answer that they can share toys, allowance, kind words, and do chores for others.* At school? *Answers might include sharing a lunch, welcoming a new child to class, or listening to a friend who seems upset.* At church? *Children might say they could welcome a new family to church, or thank their teachers and church leaders for teaching them about Jesus.*

What wonderful ways to help! You certainly seem to have loving and kind hearts!

Now I'll open this last bag. Inside is something for each of you! *Give each child a heart sticker.* When you look at your heart sticker, remember that when you show love and kindness to others, you're actually giving God a gift.

Let's hold our heart stickers over our hearts and say a simple prayer. ♥ "Dear God, please help us to have giving hearts, and please help us to be kind to others. In Jesus' name, amen." ♥

Theme:
God is everywhere.

Bible Reference:
Psalm 33:13-14

Simple Supplies:
You'll need a Bible,
tortillas, pocket bread, and French
bread. Place each kind of bread in a separate brown
paper bag. Also in each bag, place some bite-size pieces of the particular bread.

How Can God Be Everywhere at One Time?

Have you ever wondered how God can be everywhere at one time? How can God hear my prayer and the prayer of someone in China at the same time? *Allow time for children to respond.* God is so incredible that it's sometimes hard for our simple minds to understand such an amazing God! But I hope today's lesson will help you understand God a little more.

Open your Bible to Psalm 33:13-14, and show children the passage. Psalm 33 says, "From heaven the Lord looks down and sees all mankind; from his dwelling place he watches all who live on earth." What a wonderful thought it is that God is everywhere enjoying the praise and worship that people all over the world are giving to him on this day!

To help us understand a little more about God being everywhere around the world at the same time, I've brought some breads from all around the world. I'll be doing some actions as I tell you about these breads. Watch me closely, and see if you can do the same actions that I do. Ready? Here we go.

Open the first bag, and take out the tortillas. Hold them up for the children to see. In this bag I have tortillas. In what countries are tortillas eaten? *Help children understand that tortillas are commonly eaten in Mexico or Latin America.*

Let's pretend we're in Mexico. The sun is rising, and the rooster is crowing in our little village. *Lead kids in saying "cock-a-doodle-doo."* Mama is getting up very early in the morning to begin cooking for the family. *Stretch your arms and yawn.* She begins mixing flour, water, and lard for our family's breakfast. *Pretend to mix and knead the dough.* She rolls out large circles of dough and cooks the tortillas over an outdoor stove. *Pretend to roll out the dough, then pretend to cook the tortillas.*

Our family enjoys the tortilla breakfast! *Rub your stomach, and pretend to eat.* Then we all walk to church together for morning worship. *Walk in place.* God hears the morning prayers of our family and smiles on us. *Make praying hands.*

Open the second bag, and take out the pocket bread. Hold it up for the children to see. In this bag I have pocket bread. In what countries is pocket bread eaten? *Help children understand that pocket bread is eaten in Egypt, Greece, Lebanon, and the Middle East.*

Pretend we're in Egypt and our mother is preparing the day's bread for our family. She mixes the flour, oil, water, yeast, and salt. *Mix the dough and knead it.* She rolls the dough out into perfect circles and bakes the bread in a wood-burning oven. *Pretend to roll out the dough, then pretend to put the bread in the oven.* The bread puffs up and is hot and ready to eat in no time. We're all so hungry!

Our family prays and thanks God for giving us such good food to eat. *Make praying hands.* Then we enjoy the wonderful fresh bread for breakfast. *Pretend to eat.* God smiles as he sees our family start our day together.

Open the last bag, and take out the French bread. Hold it up for the children to see. In this bag I have French bread. In what country is French bread eaten? *Explain that French bread comes from France and is common in other European countries as well.*

Pretend that we're in a bakery in a little French country village. Our father is awake before the sun rises. *Stretch and yawn.* He mixes the flour and other ingredients to make the bread for all the neighbors in the village. *Mix the dough and knead it.* People will buy bread from him to eat for breakfast before going to church this morning. *Make praying hands.*

God sees people all over the world preparing themselves to worship him. *Put hand over eyes like God looking down.* God is happy to give us good things to eat, and God is happy when we praise him.

Now let's sample these breads we know so much about! But before we do, let's thank God and praise him for his goodness. Let's pray. ❤ Dear God, thank you for this food, and for all of the other wonderful blessings you give us. We praise you for being everywhere and seeing everyone at the same time. You truly are amazing! Thank you for loving us. In Jesus' name, amen. ❤

As we enjoy these breads, let's remember what the Bible says in the book of Psalms: "From heaven the Lord looks down and sees all mankind; from his dwelling place he watches all who live on earth." *Have three children help pass out small pieces of the different breads for children to sample.*

These breads are eaten all over the world. God sees the people making these breads every day. From heaven he sees them and he sees us. He sees all of us eating bread, playing, sleeping, learning, and laughing. He hears all our prayers. He helps all of us with our needs. God is everywhere!

This week as you eat bread, remember the stories of people from around the world and think about how God sees everyone. He's with everyone at the same time. Our God is amazing!

If you have enough bread bites left over, let children each take a few pieces with them to share with congregation and family members.

Theme:
God is all-powerful.

Bible Reference:
2 Chronicles 20:6

Simple Supplies:
You'll need a Bible, a hair dryer, an extension cord, and inexpensive pocket combs.

Can anyone think of an energy source that doesn't cost any money to run and will never run out? *Let kids contribute ideas.* How about the wind?

Long ago, before there were big power companies, farmers used windmills to accomplish all kinds of tasks on their farms. Today, big windmills are set up in rows in some valleys. They use the power of the wind to help provide power for entire cities!

I brought something with me today that can help make wind. It's my hair dryer! *Take out the hair dryer, and plug it in to the nearest outlet.*

When I turn on this hair dryer, I'll demonstrate its wind power by blowing your hair. *Turn the hair dryer on cool, but on high speed, and gently blow each child's hair. Make sure not to get too close to any child's face, and don't persist if a child is reluctant to have his or her hair blown.*

Now I want you all to fold your hands and put your hands in your lap. I'm going to blow your hair again, but this time, try to keep your hair from blowing. You can't move your hands, though. You'll just have to think really hard and tell your hair not to blow in the wind. Ready? Let's try it.

Blow kids' hair again, while encouraging them to think hard about it—to try really hard to keep their hair still!

How did that work? Were you able to command your hair to resist the wind power of the dryer? That hair dryer was pretty powerful, wasn't it? Your hair wasn't able to resist it.

But you know, there's a much greater power than this hair dryer, or the big windmills, or even anything else on earth. That's the power of God!

Open your Bible to 2 Chronicles 20:6, and show children the passage. In the book of Second Chronicles, the Bible says: "O Lord, God...You rule over all the kingdoms of the nations. Power and might are in your hand, and no one can withstand you."

Allow children time to respond to each of the following questions. What can God do that people can't do? What do you think is the most powerful thing on earth? Are those powerful things more powerful than God? When is a time you saw God's power at work in nature? When is a time you saw God's power at work in your own life or in your family?

I'm going to give each of you a small comb to take home with you. Each time you dry and comb your hair, remember the power of my hair dryer. And then remember that just as your hair couldn't resist the hair dryer's wind power, the Bible says that nothing can resist the power of God. What a mighty God we serve! Let's all clap and cheer for our powerful God! *Lead children in clapping and cheering for God. Then give each child a comb.*

❤ As we go back to out seats, let's sing a song as our closing prayer to God! *Lead children in singing "What a Mighty God We Serve." Invite the congregation to join in the singing as children return to their seats.*

What a mighty God we serve.
What a mighty God we serve.
Angels bow before him,
Heaven and earth adore him;
What a mighty God we serve. ❤

Does God Laugh?

Theme:
God gives us his joy.

Bible Reference:
Zephaniah 3:17

Simple Supplies:

You'll need a Bible, Laffy Taffy candy (scored with a table knife before you meet, if possible), and an attention-getting device such as a whistle or bell. (If you can't find Laffy Taffy, have kids bend red licorice into a smile.)

Have you ever noticed how each one of us laughs differently? Let's try some different laughs together. Some people just giggle, like this. *Giggle, then have kids imitate your giggle.* Some people really belly laugh, like this. *Lead kids in a belly laugh.* And some people have a really tiny little laugh, like this. *Lead kids in a small, tittering laugh.*

I have a challenging game for you today. It's called the HA-HA Game. *Giggle as you tell kids the rules.* I'll start with a single HA!, then the person on my right will respond with HA-HA! The next person has to say HA-HA-HA! Each one of you will add a "HA" when I point to you. Are you ready? Let's laugh! *Play the laughing game with the kids, playing faster and faster until the whole group dissolves in laughter.*

Use your attention-getting device to help kids calm down. You know, laughter is a strange thing. It's contagious! We catch it from the people around us. We catch joy in the same way—by being around other people who are joyful. *Open your Bible to Zephaniah 3:17, and show children the verse.* Listen to what the Bible says in the book of Zephaniah:

"The Lord your God is with you,
he is mighty to save.
He will take great delight in you,
he will quiet you with his love,
he will rejoice over you with singing."

How about that? God is rejoicing about us! We make him feel happy enough to rejoice! Isn't that wonderful? God gives us his joy, and he wants us to pass that joy on to others. To help you pass God's joy to others, I have a piece of Laffy Taffy to share with all you great laughers. Take it and share it with someone who makes you happy! *Distribute the candy.*

Let's thank God for giving us his joy. ❤ Dear God, thank you for your gift of joy and laughter. Help us to celebrate your joy and to pass it on to others. In Jesus' name, amen. ❤

Theme:
*We can trust
God's plans.*

Bible Reference:
Psalm 139:13; Jeremiah 29:11

How Does God Know the future?

Simple Supplies:

You'll need a Bible, a small paper bag, and three separate plastic sandwich bags. The first plastic bag should contain five one-inch squares of red construction paper. The second plastic bag should contain five one-inch squares of slick white paper, such as index cards.

You'll need to be able to tell the color of the paper square by the feel of the paper, not by looking at it. The third bag should contain a one-inch blue square for each child you expect.

I thought we'd talk a little today about predicting the future. People on television claim every day that they can tell you what your future holds with just a telephone call. Some people say they can tell you what will happen to you by the way certain cards are dealt. Some people say they can tell the future by looking at your hand. But none of those things are true.

I want to show you something. We'll do an experiment about telling the future.

I have some red squares of paper that I'm going to place in this bag. *Place the red squares in the paper bag.* I also have some white squares. *Place the white squares in the same paper bag.*

Now there are an equal number of red squares and white squares in the bag, so we'll have an equal chance of pulling out either a red square or a white square. Right?

I'm going to ask a volunteer to reach in and grab a square. We'll try to tell the future by guessing what color will come out. Ready? *Have a child reach in and grasp a paper square without removing it.* Who thinks it will be white? red? *Let the child reveal the color. Repeat the same process a number of times, letting different children choose the paper square.*

How many of you guessed right every time? You know, I can tell you the right color before I look at it! Watch. I'll even keep my eyes closed. *Close your eyes, and choose a paper square. Have the kids guess which color it will be, then state what color it is, and reveal the square.* Was I right? *Repeat the process several times, guessing correctly each time.*

How did I do that? *Let children respond.* You know, I have a secret, and it's not peeking! And I can't tell the future, either. No one can tell the future, except God!

I made this game. And I had a plan from the beginning. Feel the red squares. *Pass several red paper squares around the group.* Now feel the white squares. *Pass several white squares around the group.*

Each time I picked out a square, I could tell by the feel of it which color it was. The red squares felt a little scratchy, and the white squares felt smooth and slick. Because I made the game, I understood everything about it, and I knew how it would work.

And it's the same with God. You see, God made you. He made the earth, and the heavens, and everything in them. He knows how everything works, and he's the only one who can tell what's going to happen next!

Only God really knows the future. That's why we can trust his plans. *Open your Bible to Psalm 139:13.* The Bible says in Psalm 139:13 that God created each of us in a special way. Listen. "For you created my inmost being; you knit me together in my mother's womb."

Turn in your Bible to Jeremiah 29:11. And the Bible says in Jeremiah 29:11: " 'For I know the plans I have for you,' declares the Lord, 'plans to prosper you and not to harm you, plans to give you hope and a future.' "

Because God created you, he knows your future, just as I knew the future in the game that I created. God doesn't guess. He has a plan for you.

Does anyone know what a blueprint is? A blueprint is a big plan that engineers use when they're building something. Just as engineers use a blueprint for building a building or a bridge, God has a sort of a blueprint for your future.

Open the bag of blue squares, and give each child one. I'm going to give each of you a blue paper square to remind you that God has a blueprint for your life.

Let's pray. ❤ Dear God, as we hold onto these blue squares, help us to remember that you made a blueprint for each of our lives. You made plans to take care of us and to give us hope. Help us to trust your plans for us, because we know you love us. Thank you. In Jesus' name, amen. ❤

Theme:
God doesn't forget his promises.

Bible Reference:
Joshua 23:14b; Hebrews 10:17b

Simple Supplies:
You'll need a Bible, a chalkboard, chalk and an eraser, plus one piece of chalk for each child. (Optional: a can of cat food, honey, hamburger buns, tuna, and a roll of paper towels in a grocery bag)

I heard a story recently about someone who had to go to the grocery story to pick up some things for a lady he was helping. She gave him the list while he was talking on his car phone, so he couldn't write anything down. He didn't want to forget, so he worked out a way to use his fingers to help him remember what to buy.

She needed five things—hamburger buns, cat food, honey, tuna, and paper towels. *If you brought the actual items, take them out of a grocery bag as you name each item.*

This is how he remembered what to buy. *Place the items back in the bag as you count them off.*

One bun, for hamburger buns. *Hold up one finger.*

Two mews, for cat food. *Hold up two fingers.*

Three trees, because paper towels come from trees. *Hold up three fingers.*

Four seashores, for tuna from the sea. *Hold up four fingers.*

Five hives, for honey from the hives. *Hold up five fingers.*

Now let's see if you can remember along with me. *Repeat the list with the children.* Give yourselves a hand for such great memory power!

Allow children to respond to each of the following questions. What kinds of things do you have to remember every day? How do you remember really important things? Is it always easy to remember things? Have you ever forgotten something important? Sometimes, even with all of the different tricks we use to try to remember, we still forget.

But God never forgets. God always remembers his promises. *Open your Bible to Joshua 23:14b.* The Bible says in Joshua 23:14: "You know with all your heart and soul that not one of all the good promises the Lord your God gave you has failed. Every promise has been fulfilled; not one has failed."

God never forgets his promises. And God's promises never fail. What promises has God made to us? *Allow children to respond.*

God promises to love us, and take care of us, and forgive us when we're sorry. And when God forgives us, he promises to forget the wrong things we've done.

Open your Bible to Hebrews 10:17b, and show children the verse. Listen to what the Bible says in Hebrews 10:17: "Their sins and lawless acts I will remember no more."

What does God say in this verse that he'll forget? *Allow children to respond, and repeat the verse for the children if they need prompting.*

Write the word "sins" on the chalkboard. When we ask for forgiveness, God erases our sins. *Erase the word from the board.* Then he forgets the sin. God chooses to forget the wrong things we do, as long as we're sorry and ask him for forgiveness. *Have a child blow the chalk dust from the eraser.*

That's another of God's promises—to forgive and forget! And God always keeps his promises!

Let's pray together. ❤ Dear God, thank you for never forgetting your promises! And thank you for choosing to forgive and forget our sins. Thank you for your love. Amen. ❤

I'm going to give each of you a piece of chalk to take home. Each time you erase a picture you've drawn with the chalk, remember God's promise to forgive and forget. And remember that God always keeps his promises! *Give each child a piece of chalk.*

Theme:
We can hear God in many ways.

Bible Reference:
John 10:3-5

Simple Supplies:
You'll need a Bible, sheep stickers or cotton balls, a cassette player, and a tape with recordings of several voices familiar to your children. You might record your own voice, your pastor's voice, or a teacher's voice.

Let's play Name That Voice! I have a tape of some people you may know. Raise your hand when you think you know who's speaking. *Play each voice on the tape. After each voice, stop the tape and allow children to guess who was speaking.*

After children have guessed who every voice belongs to, play the tape again, and reveal the real owner of each voice.

How were you able to recognize the voices on the tape? *Allow children to answer.* Exactly! You knew the voices because you had spent time with the person behind the voice. In the book of John, Jesus tells us about sheep who know their shepherd's voice. *Hold up your Bible, then open it to John 10:3-5.* Listen to what the Bible says in John 10:3-5: "The watchman opens the gate for [the shepherd], and the sheep listen to his voice. He calls his own sheep by name and leads them out. When he has brought out all his own, he goes on ahead of them, and his sheep follow him because they know his voice. But they will never follow a stranger; in fact, they will run away from him because they do not recognize a stranger's voice."

Who do you suppose is the shepherd the Bible is talking about? That's right. Jesus is our shepherd, and we're his sheep. Jesus knows our names, and we follow him because we know his voice. Jesus knows us, and we know him, and he always goes ahead of us to lead us!

I have a sheep sticker (or cotton ball) for each of you to remind you to listen for the voice of Jesus, your shepherd. *Give each child a sheep sticker or a cotton ball.*

As we close in prayer today, I'll say a line of the prayer, and I want you to say, "We'll be listening." Are you ready? Here we go.

♥ Dear God, please speak to us through your Word. (We'll be listening.)
Speak to us as we pray. (We'll be listening.)
When we hear your voice, Jesus, we'll follow. (We'll be listening.)
Amen. ♥

Theme:
God can speak to anyone, in any language.

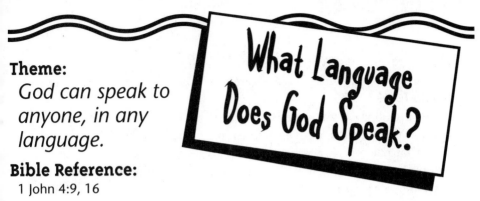

What Language Does God Speak?

Bible Reference:
1 John 4:9, 16

Simple Supplies:
You'll need a Bible and Hershey's Kisses or candy valentine hearts.

I have an especially important message for you this morning, so I want you to listen closely. Here it is: qanta munani (con-ta mu-NA-ni). *Look at the children as though you are expecting them to respond.* Oh. I guess no one here speaks Quechua. It's a Bolivian Indian dialect.

Let me try this: Ta gra agam ort (ta gra AY-gum ort). Same message, just a different language. No one here speaks Gaelic either, I see.

How about "Ich liebe dich" (ich leeb-eh dich)? That's German.

Je t'aime (zh tem)? That's French.

Te amo (tay ah-mo)? That's Spanish.

How about this? *Hold your middle finger and ring finger down while extending pinkie, forefinger, and thumb.* That's American Sign Language.

Does anyone know what I'm trying to say? *Allow children to respond.*

I was trying to say, "I love you." There are so many different ways to say the same thing, aren't there? There are hundreds of different languages in the world. We couldn't possibly learn them all, could we?

Do you think God speaks every language on earth? *Let children respond. Then hold up your Bible.* We know from the Bible that God speaks to us with the language of love. *Turn to 1 John 4:9 and 16.* Listen to what the Bible says in the book of First John: "This is how God showed his love among us: He sent his one and only Son into the world that we might live through him...God is love."

Some people say that love is the universal language—it needs no words at all. Since God is love, we know he speaks the language of love, right? What are some ways God shows his love to us? *Let children respond.* What are some ways we can show God's love to others?

27

Can you think of any ways to show love without words? *Allow children to respond. If they need prompting, suggest such ways as hugging, handshakes, or pats on the back.*

Those are all good answers! We might show God's love with hugs, smiles, pats on the back, or even handshakes. Choose a partner, and turn and face that person. Now think of a way to show God's love to your partner without words. When I count to three, let's all show God's love. Ready? One...two...three...show!

For extra fun, ask the members of the congregation to join the children in finding partners and wordlessly showing God's love.

Great job, everyone! You really showed God's love! *Take out the candy treats.* What do these candy treats say to you? *Let children answer.* What I'm trying to say with these candy treats is that I love you and so does God!

I do love you, and I want you to take one of these candies as a reminder that God's language of love is understood by everyone!

But first, let's hold hands as a sign of love as we pray together. ♥ Dear God, we know you can speak any language to anyone in the whole wide world. Thank you for speaking to us with your love. Please help us speak your love to others. Amen. ♥

Give each child a candy treat to keep and several treats to share with members of the congregation and parents.

Theme:
God communi-
cates with us in
many ways.

Bible Reference:
Psalm 29:3-4

Simple Supplies:
You'll need a Bible and postcards.

Today we're going to talk about talking. That sounds pretty simple, doesn't it?

Allow children to respond to the following questions. When you have a message to give someone, how to you pass that message along? How many different ways can you think of to communicate a message to someone? Usually we use our voices to communicate what we want to say. But there are other ways!

Have children form two groups where they are sitting. To one group, whisper the word "cookies," then have them communicate this word to the other group without using words. When that message has been communicated, give the other group a chance to communicate the message "love," to the first group.

Great job! You all found ways to communicate your messages! We learned that we can communicate without using our voices. *Allow children time to respond to the following questions.* How do you think God communicates with us? Have you ever heard God's voice?

God communicates with us in many ways. One way is by using his voice. The Bible tells us of people who actually heard God's voice. Moses heard God's voice in a burning bush. And Job heard God's voice in a storm. *Open your Bible to Psalm 29:3-4.*

And Psalm 29:3-4 describes God's voice like this: "The voice of the Lord is over the waters...The voice of the Lord is powerful; the voice of the Lord is majestic." What does this passage make you think God's voice sounds like?

Some people believe they hear God's voice telling them what they should do. But most people never hear God's voice as you're hearing my voice right now. Instead, God communicates to us through other different ways. What other ways do you think God uses to communicate with us? *Allow children to respond.*

Thanks for those answers! God uses prayer as a way for us to talk back and forth to each other. And God uses other Christians to help and teach us the things we need to know.

God also uses all of the beautiful parts of nature to give us a wonderful world to live in, and to remind us how much he loves us. And most of all, God speaks to us through the Bible. The Bible is God's Word that he gave to us to help us learn about him, and about his Son, and about how he wants us to live. The Bible is like God's special letter, just to us.

Give each child a postcard. This card can do two things. First, it can remind you of God's letter to you, the Bible. Second, you can write a message or draw a picture for someone else this week. Use this card this week to remind that person of God's love! Now let's pray before we go.

❤ Dear God, I'm glad we can talk to you. Thank you for listening. I'm also glad you communicate to us in many different ways. Thank you for giving us the Bible as one of your messages to us. Amen. ❤

Theme:
We don't know what God looks like, but we know what God IS like.

Bible Reference:
John 1:18

Simple Supplies:
You'll need a Bible and a box of oyster crackers.

What does it mean when someone says, "A penny for your thoughts?" *Allow children to respond.*

Today we're going to play a game called A Penny for Your Thoughts. *Have one child stand.* Because each of your thoughts is very important to me, when you tell me how you know (child's name), I'll give each of you one of these penny-shaped crackers. When you see (child's name) on Sunday morning, how do you know that's who this person is?

After several children respond, let the child who is standing sit down with the group. Then give every child a cracker.

Now let's play another round of A Penny for Your Thoughts. You may have a penny cracker for your thoughts if you can tell me how I would recognize God if I needed to meet him in the supermarket. What would he look like? What would he sound like? How would I know that it's God? *Kids may offer several ideas. Encourage them to tell you how they would know that particular detail about God.*

Why do you think it's so hard to describe what God looks like? Has anyone ever actually seen God? *Open your Bible to John 1:18.* The Bible says in John 1:18: "No one has ever seen God, but God the One and Only, who is at the Father's side, has made him known."

So we don't actually know what God looks like, but we do know what God is like, because Jesus shows us just that! God sent Jesus down to earth to help us learn about God and to give us a way to live with God. If we believe in Jesus, we can live with God forever!

Because of Jesus, we've been able to learn lots of things about God. What have you learned about God so far? *Allow children to respond.*

That's great! We know that God is always with us and that God will always love us. How can we learn even more about God? *Let children answer.*

Terrific! By going to church, and reading the Bible, and praying, and talking to other Christians, we can learn lots and lots more about God!

Someday, we'll know what God looks like. I'm sure of it! We'll see God face to face in heaven. Won't it be great to know what God looks like, after learning so much about what God is like?

Let's close in prayer to our wonderful God. 💜 Dear God, you know our every thought. You don't need to give us a penny for our thoughts! Thank you for showing us what you're like through your Word and through your Son, Jesus. We're looking forward to seeing you face to face someday in heaven! Amen. 💜

Give each child a few more crackers. Take these penny crackers with you to share with someone in the congregation. Go up to that person right now and say, "A penny for your thoughts!" Then ask that person to tell you one thing he or she knows about God. After the person answers, you may give him or her a cracker!

Theme:
We can show others what God is like.

Bible Reference:
Matthew 25:35-36, 40b

Simple Supplies:

You'll need a Bible, a baby doll wrapped in a blanket, a disposable diaper, a bar of soap or a bottle of baby shampoo, a baby bottle, and O-shaped cereal.

Lay out all the baby supplies. Hold the baby doll in your arms. Let's pretend that this is a real baby. *Begin gently passing the baby to the child next to you.* When you get a chance to hold the baby, tell the others in the group what you would need to do to take care of this baby.

Make sure that each child has an opportunity to hold the baby and contribute an answer.

Babies need a lot of care. What would you think if you saw a real baby who's happy, and healthy, and dressed in nice warm clothes, and wrapped in a soft blanket, and who has a full bottle? How would you think that baby's parents feel about that baby? How could you tell? *Allow children to respond.*

Even if we couldn't see the baby's parents, we could tell that they loved the baby by the way they took care of it. It's the same way with God. Even though we can't see God, we can tell that he loves people by the way he takes care of them. How does God take care of people? How does God take care of you?

We can tell what God is like by the way he acts. And we can show others what God is like by the way we act, too! Did you know that when we take care of others, we're actually showing them what God is like? How can our actions show God to others?

We all know how important it is to feed babies (and kids too!) so let's munch on some cereal while I read to you from the Bible. *Give each child a small handful of cereal.*

Open your Bible to Matthew 25:35-36, 40b. Listen to what Jesus says in Matthew 25: "For I was hungry and you gave me something to eat, I was thirsty and you gave me something to drink, I was a stranger and you invited me in, I needed clothes and you clothed me, I was sick and you looked after me, I was in prison and you came to visit me...I tell you the truth, whatever you did for one of the least of these brothers of mine, you did for me."

What do you think Jesus means in this passage? How is giving clothes to the needy like giving clothes to Jesus? *Allow children to respond.*

God is so kind! Not only does God take care of us in ways we may not even notice each day, but he sends people like our parents or grandparents to take care of us. God is loving. He gives us people who love us. When they take care of us, just as parents take care of their babies, they're helping God. When they love us, they're showing God's love to us.

Let's pray a show-me prayer. When we pray, you may keep your eyes open and show me what God is like by acting out each part, just the way I do.

❤ Dear God, help me to be kind, just like you. *Pat the back of the child next to you.* Help me to be loving, just like you. *Cross your arms in front of you, like you're giving yourself a hug.* Help me to help others. *Shake hands with a child near you.* Thank you for loving us and taking care of us. *Clap hands.* Amen! ❤

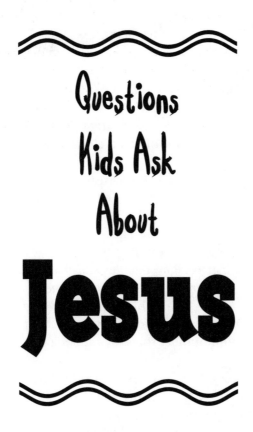

Questions
Kids Ask
About

Jesus

Theme:

It's important to study and learn.

Bible Reference:

Luke 2:46-47

Simple Supplies:

You'll need a Bible and balloons.

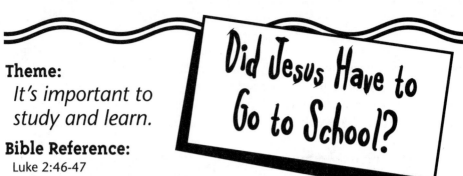
Did Jesus Have to Go to School?

oday we're going to talk about learning. What do you think it means to be a Learner? How many of you are Learners? *Allow children to respond.* Let's see if that's true.

I have several questions to ask. If you really are a Learner, you should be able to tell me the answers. There's no need to raise your hand—just shout out your answers.

Hold up one balloon. Each time you answer one of my questions, I'll blow up this balloon a little more. Ready? Here we go! *Allow children to respond to each of the following questions. Blow into the balloon after each question. When the balloon is full, tie it off, and hold it until later in the message.*

Here's question number one: Who is the pastor of our church?

Now here's question number two: What town is our church in?

Next comes question number three: What book can we read to learn more about Jesus?

Well, you do all seem to be Learners! Good job! But none of you came into the world knowing all those answers, did you? How did you know the answers?

Let's try one more question. Here's question number four: Did Jesus have to go to school? *Let kids answer in any way they wish.*

Those are all interesting answers. Let's think about what we know from the Bible. We know that Jewish boys in Jesus' time were taught by rabbis at the temple, so Jesus probably went to school.

In fact, the Bible tells us of a specific time Jesus went to school. *Open your Bible to Luke 2:46-47.* Listen to what the Bible says in the book of Luke: "After three days they found him in the temple courts, sitting among the teachers, listening to them and asking them questions. Everyone who heard him was amazed at his understanding and his answers."

Jesus knew God in a closer way than any of the teachers, because God was his Father who sent him to earth. But Jesus also knew that it's important to be in God's house. He knew that learning about God is important, even though he was still a child. Jesus surrounded himself with people who loved learning about God, and he showed us that it's important to study and learn about God.

Hold up the balloon. Just as this balloon grew bigger and bigger as you answered each of my questions, each year that we go to school we grow taller and bigger. That's easy to see. It's not as easy to see that our minds are growing too!

It's important that we study and learn so our minds will grow full with knowledge. And it's even more important for us to study and learn about God. What are some ways we can learn more about God?

Thanks for those answers! We can pray, and read the Bible, and come to church. We can become Learners and be filled with knowledge about God, just as this balloon became filled with air.

Hand the balloon to the nearest child. As we pass this balloon from person to person, I'd like each of you to tell one thing you've learned about God.

Give each child a chance to respond. Since you're all such bright Learners today, I'll bet you know what we're going to do to close our time together. That's right! We're going to pray!

❤ Dear Jesus, you showed us that it's important to study and learn. Not only do we need to go to school, but we also need to come to church to learn more about you. Be with us this week as we learn. Fill our minds and let us become Learners who will please you. Amen. ❤

Give each child a balloon. Take these balloons home with you. When you blow up the balloon, remember that you can become filled with knowledge about God!

Theme:
*God is our
forever friend.*

Bible Reference:
Isaiah 41:10

Simple Supplies:

You'll need a Bible and Gummi Savers candies.

Before you begin, slide one of the Gummi Savers onto one of your fingers. I have a ring here that reminds me of my best friend.

Give each child a candy to place on his or her finger. Think about your best friend as you slide the ring on your finger. What makes your best friend more special than any other friend you have? *Allow children to respond.*

Then *wiggle your finger with the candy ring on it and pretend to admire the ring.* Every time I look down at this ring, I'm reminded of my best friend. I'm reminded that I need to talk to my best friend. What kinds of things do you talk about with your best friend? *Let children answer.*

Have the kids remove their rings and look at them.

This ring reminds me to talk to my best friend for lots of reasons. The shape of this ring reminds me of my friend because it's a circle without a beginning or an end. And my best friend has always loved me. Just as I can't find the beginning or end of this circle, I can't find the time my friend began loving me. And my best friend will never stop loving me, either. It's like a circle of love!

Have the kids gently bend the Gummi Savers back and forth.

Look at how strong these rings are. My best friend is also very strong. Even when I get mad and say mean things to him, he never falls apart. He's always the same. He's always my friend, just like a best friend should be.

Have the kids slide the Gummi Savers back on their fingers.

Just like this ring, my best friend is just the right size. No matter how old I am, or how big my finger gets, my best friend still "fits." I can always count on my friend to know what I need and to listen whenever I talk to him. He always knows what's in my heart. Do you think your best friend knows what's in your heart? How do you know?

Before you guess who my best friend is, I'll give you one more clue. My best friend was also Jesus' best friend. He came with me to church today.

Open your Bible to Isaiah 41:10. Let me introduce my best friend to you by reading Isaiah 41:10: "So do not fear, for I am with you; do not be dismayed, for I am your God. I will strengthen you and help you; I will uphold you with my righteous right hand."

Do you think it's possible that we share best friends? Have you guessed who my best friend is? That's right, it's God! God is my forever friend!

Have kids hold up their hands with the candy rings. You know, I still need to talk to my best friend today. Would you like to talk to him, too?

Let's pray. ❤ Dear God, you really are our best friend. You are always there for us. You're always strong. You're always just our size. We know that we can count on you to know what's in our hearts and to love us all the time. Thank you! In Jesus' name, amen. ❤

We can always count on God to be our best friend. Remember to talk to him today at least once before you eat your candy ring. I'm going to give you another candy to take with you. Give the second candy to someone and tell that person about your best, forever friend!

Theme:

Even when he was on earth, Jesus was never separated from God.

Bible Reference:

John 17:22

Simple Supplies:

You'll need a Bible, craft sticks, and adhesive tape.

As the children are coming forward, give each child a craft stick. Without tipping your head back, try to balance this stick on your nose. *Let the kids try to balance the sticks on their noses.* How easy was it to balance the craft stick on your nose without moving your head back? That was really hard, wasn't it?

Allow children to answer and discuss the following questions. What are some other hard or difficult things you've ever had to do? When you do something very hard, how do you feel after you're finished? Why do we sometimes not want to do hard things?

You know, Jesus did some things that were very hard. We can learn a lot from Jesus' life. He left his Father in heaven, his real home, and came to earth. How do you think you would feel if you had to leave your home and go somewhere far away? What do you do if you or your parents have to be away from each other for very long? How do you stay in touch?

Jesus kept in touch with his Father too. How do you suppose he did that?

That's right! Jesus talked to God in prayer. One prayer that Jesus prayed is recorded in the book of John. *Open your Bible to John 17:22.* In this prayer, Jesus talked to God about lots of things. Jesus talked about his disciples, and about the people like us who would believe in him later, and about how he felt about the work God had given him to do on earth.

Listen as I read from the Bible. In verse 22, Jesus says, "I have given them the glory that you gave me, that they may be one as we are one."

You see, even though Jesus was away from his home, he was never really away from his Father. He said that he was one with his Father. They talked all the time. When is your favorite time to talk to God?

Jesus was never alone, because he knew his Father loved him and talked to him all the time. And you're never really alone either, because your heavenly Father loves you, and you can always talk to God.

Show children how to gently bend their craft sticks back and forth. When you bend your stick, it looks pretty weak, doesn't it? Don't try it, but if you bend it too hard, it may even break. Your stick is weak because it's all alone.

Give each child another craft stick and a piece of adhesive tape. Show the children how to tape their two craft sticks together, making them into one.

When these two sticks are taped together, they're much stronger. They become like one. That's how it is with you and God. God will stay with you, no matter what. No matter what hard thing you may have to do, he'll stay right by you. And since you're so close to each other, you can always talk and stay in touch with each other.

Let's stay in touch with God right now.

♥ Dear Jesus, you did an amazingly hard thing when you left heaven to do God's will on earth. Thank you for loving us that much. Thank you for making it possible for us to stay in touch with God. Remind us to always stick very close to our heavenly Father. In Jesus' name, amen. ♥

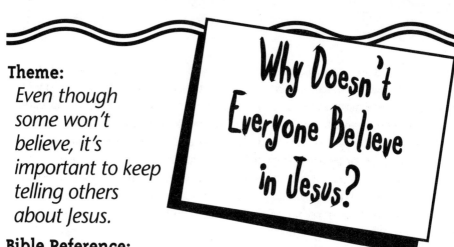

Theme:
Even though some won't believe, it's important to keep telling others about Jesus.

Bible Reference:
Matthew 28:19-20

Simple Supplies:
You'll need a Bible and a bag or box with enough small pieces of unusual fruit (such as mango, pomegranate, or papaya) to serve twice the number of children you expect.

oday I have a special gift for you. It's something to eat. Best of all, it's free. You may each take a piece if you would like.

Open your bag, and offer a piece of the fruit to each child. Some may not want any. That's OK. Take a bite of a piece of fruit yourself. Pass the bag around again, and offer kids seconds.

Each of you was offered a free gift today: a taste of fruit. Why did you decide to take or not take the fruit? *Allow children to respond.* Tasting this unusual fruit is a little bit like believing in Jesus. In the same way, God offers us the free gift of his Son.

Whether we choose to try new foods or not isn't important. But it is important to believe in Jesus. But there are some people who make the choice not to take God's free gift of Jesus. They don't believe in Jesus. Have you ever known someone who doesn't believe in Jesus? That person's reasons for not accepting God's free gift may be much like someone's reasons for not trying a new food. Maybe the person has never even heard of the new food! And maybe someone is afraid to try believing in Jesus because they might not know anything about him. That's where we can help!

Open your Bible to Matthew 28:19-20. In Matthew 28:19-20, Jesus says, "Therefore go and make disciples of all nations, baptizing them in the name of the Father and of the Son and of the Holy Spirit, and teaching them to obey everything I have commanded you. And surely I am with you always, to the very end of the age."

The Bible says that it's our job to keep telling others about the free gift of

Jesus, even though some people may not ever believe. We can tell people in our neighborhood. We can tell people in school. We can even tell people in other parts of the world, who may never have even heard the name of Jesus.

Give children time to respond to the following questions. How can you tell about the free gift of Jesus in your neighborhood? How can you help tell about the free gift of Jesus in faraway places?

It's always good to tell others about Jesus! Sometimes you may need to tell about the free gift of Jesus more than once, just as I offered you the fruit more than once. The important thing is to keep telling, so that people know God's gift of Jesus is always available.

Let's pray together. ♥ Dear God, thank you for the free gift of your only Son, Jesus. Help us to share your gift with others by telling them about Jesus. Amen. ♥

Offer kids another taste of fruit as they leave.

Theme:
Jesus wants us to honor God's house.

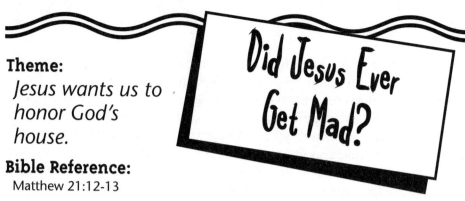

Did Jesus Ever Get Mad?

Bible Reference:
Matthew 21:12-13

Simple Supplies:
You'll need a Bible and heart stickers.

Begin *this children's sermon by bounding up to the front of the room, full of energy. You may even want to dress the energetic part by wearing exercise clothing. Lead the kids in several jumping jacks before beginning the message.*

I've been getting ready for church! How about you? Did you get ready to come to church today? What are some things you do each week to get ready for church?

We can also get ready for church by doing some church aerobics. Let's practice doing some church aerobics, even though we're already here.

First, we can do ten neck rolls to prepare our heads for bowing in prayer. *Lead the children in stretching their necks from left to right and from front to back.*

Another helpful church exercise is the deep knee bend. This is important to get us ready for the sitting and standing we'll do during the church service. *Lead the kids in ten deep knee bends, then encourage the kids to do one last deep knee bend and sit down.*

Finally, it's important to practice the finger flex before church! This exercise gets our hands ready to shake the hands of others. *Lead the kids in flexing their fingers, one by one, several times.*

These church aerobics can help us prepare ourselves for coming to church each week. But there's one last exercise we need to do to help us get ready to honor God in his holy place. We need to exercise our hearts. *Give each child a heart sticker to place over his or her heart.*

The Bible tells us of a time when the people hadn't prepared their hearts to worship God or honor his house, the temple. They hadn't done their church aerobics! In fact, they were using God's house like a store to sell things. This made Jesus very mad.

Open your Bible to Matthew 21:12-13. Listen to what the Bible says: "Jesus entered the temple area and drove out all who were buying and selling there. He overturned the tables of the money changers and the benches of those selling doves. 'It is written,' he said to them, 'My house will be called a house of prayer,' but you are making it a 'den of robbers.' "

Jesus wants us to honor God's house. Each week when we come to church, we need to prepare to worship God. We need to be ready to honor God in his house. What things can you do to prepare your hearts for worship?

Let's practice some more of our church aerobics. Let's bow our heads, open our hearts, and pray to Jesus. ❤ Dear Jesus, help us to remember that we are coming to an important event when we enter your house. Prepare us to worship and to open our hearts to honor you. Amen. ❤

Take your heart stickers home with you, and put them in your Bibles as a reminder to prepare your heart for worship each week.

Theme:

Jesus came to be just like us.

Bible Reference:

Hebrews 4:15

Simple Supplies:

You'll need a Bible and pieces of aluminum foil wrapped around small cardboard squares (one for each child).

Let's play a game called Just Like Me. We don't need to say anything during this game; just follow what I do and you'll be playing the game. *Tap your head, raise your arms, stand up, sit down, or do any actions you choose. Have the children mimic your actions. Then have the children sit down.*

You all did so well! You acted just as I did! Did you know that Jesus came down from heaven, into this world, to be just like us? He came into this world as a little baby and worked as a carpenter when he was growing up. And he had friends just like us. Jesus was just like us, except he never did anything wrong.

Open your Bible to Hebrews 4:15. The Bible tells us about Jesus in the book of Hebrews. Listen: "For we do not have a high priest who is unable to sympathize with our weaknesses, but we have one who has been tempted in every way, just as we are—yet was without sin."

Jesus can understand all of our feelings, because he came to be just like us. He knows what it feels like to hurt, and to be sad, and to get angry. And he understands all the other feelings we have. But Jesus never sinned. He is God, but he came to be just like us.

Give each child a foil-wrapped piece of cardboard. Look into your foil mirror. Use your mirror to remind you that Jesus came into this world to be just like us. But Jesus was so much more than us! He was God in human form.

Jesus became like us because he loves us. He came to give us his example to follow. He loves us so much that he left heaven to give us a way to live with God forever.

And Jesus wants us to try to be like him. He wants us to act the way he showed us, without sinning. It's kind of like playing Just Like Me using Jesus as our guide! How can you be more like Jesus? *Let children respond.*

Look at your reflections in the foil as we pray. ❤ Dear Jesus, thank you for being God's Son, and showing us how we can be like you. Help us to be reflections of you in everything we do and say. Amen. ❤

Theme:
Jesus was perfect.

Bible Reference:
Hebrews 7:26, 27b

Simple Supplies:
You'll need a Bible and a large, perfect-looking cluster of grapes.

When Jesus was your age, do you think he ever spilled his milk? Have you ever spilled your milk? Have you ever made any other mistakes? Would you like to share what happened? *You may want to describe a mistake you've made first. Others may feel more comfortable joining in the discussion after you've shared a mistake you've made.*

Well, we've all made mistakes, that's for sure! None of us is perfect. Jesus was the only perfect person to have ever lived on the earth. *Show children the cluster of grapes.* Look at these grapes. Each grape looks just like all the other grapes in the bunch, doesn't it? What are some ways we might be like these grapes? *Kids might answer that God made us and that we grow.* How are we different from these grapes? Did God make us all look alike? Are we all the same inside?

We're all different, just the way God meant for us to be. One thing we do have in common, though, is that we've all made mistakes. We all have sinned. Jesus is the only one who never sinned.

Open your Bible to Hebrews 7:26, 27b. Listen to what the Bible says in the book of Hebrews: "Such a high priest meets our need—one who is holy, blameless, pure, set apart from sinners, exalted above the heavens...He sacrificed for their sins once for all when he offered himself."

The Bible tells that only Jesus is perfect. Only Jesus is without sin. There's a difference between making a mistake and sinning. Spilling your milk by accident is a mistake. Knocking your milk glass over on purpose because you're mad is wrong. We don't know if Jesus ever accidentally spilled his milk. But we do know that Jesus never did anything wrong. And we do know that Jesus loves us, even though we aren't perfect. Even though we sometimes make mistakes, and even though we sometimes sin, we know that Jesus still loves us. In fact, we know that Jesus loved us so much that he was willing to take on our sins so that we can have forgiveness.

Give each child a grape from the cluster. Let's pray. ♥ Dear Jesus, thank you for making each one of us different, just as you did these grapes. And thank you for loving us, even though we're not perfect. Thank you for loving us, even though we make mistakes. Amen. ♥

Theme:
God loves us, even when we do wrong things.

Bible Reference:
Romans 8:38-39

Simple Supplies:
You'll need a Bible and round binder rings. In advance, securely connect two binder rings together for each child.

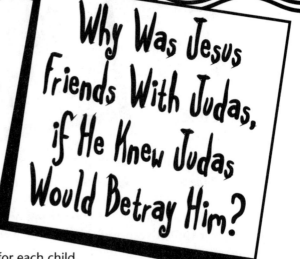

Why Was Jesus Friends With Judas, if He Knew Judas Would Betray Him?

Do any of you have a dog or cat or another pet that you love? Tell me a little about your pet. *Give children a few moments to talk about their pets. Then let them answer the following questions.*

How would you feel if that pet were to tear up a piece of furniture or your favorite toy? When your pet does something wrong, do you stop loving your pet? Even when our animals do the wrong things, we still love them, don't we?

Love is bigger than a broken toy. When we love our pets, we may be disappointed or even angry at something bad they do, but we never stop loving them.

When was the last time you did something wrong? Were you punished? How do you know your parents love you, even when they punish you? *Allow children to respond.*

Thanks for those answers! Even when we disappoint our parents or make them angry when we do wrong things, they still love us. In fact, if they didn't love us, they wouldn't care what we did.

It's the same way with Jesus. Jesus loves us even when we do wrong things. I'll give you a good example.

Do you remember the story in the Bible about Judas? Judas was a friend of Jesus', but Judas was the one to turn Jesus over to the Roman soldiers so they could arrest him. Some people wonder how Jesus could have been friends with Judas when Jesus knew that Judas would be mean to him.

Even though Jesus knew Judas would do something very wrong, Jesus still loved Judas! Let me show you something about Jesus' love.

Have two children volunteer to help you. Hold hands with one child, then ask the other to break your hands apart. If the child cannot pull your hands apart, ask for other volunteers to help until you've broken your handhold.

No matter how hard I hold hands with someone, there's always a way to break us apart. But God's love is something we can't ever be broken away from. *Open your Bible to Romans 8:38-39.* The Bible explains this kind of love in Romans 8:38-39. Listen: "For I am convinced that neither death nor life, neither angels nor demons, neither the present nor the future, nor any powers, neither height nor depth, nor anything else in all creation, will be able to separate us from the love of God that is in Christ Jesus our Lord."

According to the Bible, what can separate us from God? *Allow children to answer.* That's right—nothing! Nothing can separate us from the love of God!

No matter how many wrong things we do, God still loves us. And that's why Jesus still loved Judas, even when Judas betrayed him. Sure, it made Jesus very sad to know his friend would do this, just as it makes your parents sad when you do something wrong. But just as your parents still love you, Jesus still loved Judas. And God still loves us, even when we do wrong things. Let's thank God for his love.

💜 Dear God, thank you for loving us no matter what we do. Thank you for having love so strong that nothing can break us away from your love! In Jesus' name, amen. 💜

Give each child a pair of connected binder rings. Look at your rings. Do you see how the two rings are connected together? That's like you and God. When you look at your rings at home, remember that nothing can separate you from the love of God!

Questions
Kids Ask
About

Heaven

Theme:
In heaven we'll have something special to do.

Bible Reference:
Revelation 5:11-14

What Is There to Play With in Heaven?

Simple Supplies:
You'll need a Bible, infant toys such as rattles and teething rings, and a washable marker. Put the infant toys in a paper bag. You may also want to ask the choir to be ready to sing a simple chorus such as "Alleluia" in harmony.

One of the best things about being a child is that you get to play with toys. I bet you all have favorite toys that you love to play with. When I was a child, my favorite toy was (name your favorite toy). I played with it for hours and hours. In the morning when I woke up, it was the first thing I looked for. And sometimes at night, I'd take it to bed with me and sleep with it. I couldn't imagine not having that toy to play with. What are your favorite toys?

Inside this bag I have some toys that some children like better than all other toys. What do you think I have in this bag? *Let a few children answer. Then pull the infant toys out of the bag and show them to the children.*

Are you surprised at these toys? Who do you think might consider these toys their favorites?

Babies love these kinds of toys! They come in colors that babies like, and they make sounds that babies like. Babies think these toys are great! But if you're not a baby you probably don't play with rattles and teething rings—you play with toys that are just right for someone your age. As we grow up, the things we like to do change.

I don't play with my (favorite toy) at all anymore. But now I have things that I like to do just as much as I liked playing with my toys when I was little.

Have you ever wondered what we'll do when we get to heaven? The Bible tells us that heaven is a wondrous place—that there won't be any sadness or crying, and that people won't ever get sick there.

The Bible also tells us that Jesus is in heaven right now, preparing a place for us. The Bible tells us all sorts of things about heaven, but it doesn't tell us too much about what we'll do there.

Open your Bible to Revelation 5:11-14. But there is one passage in the very last book of the Bible that tells us what heaven will be like. It tells us a little part of what we'll do. A man named John wrote the book, and first he talks about the angels.

This is what John wrote in the Bible about heaven: "Then I looked and heard the voice of many angels, numbering thousands upon thousands, and ten thousand times ten thousand. They encircled the throne and the living creatures and the elders."

Wow! Thousands and thousands of angels. Let's flutter our fingers to show how many angels there were. *Have the children flutter their fingers.*

"In a loud voice they sang: 'Worthy is the Lamb, who was slain, to receive power and wealth and wisdom and strength and honor and glory and praise!" When they say the Lamb, they mean Jesus. The angels in heaven praise God.

Our turn is coming up next. Listen to what John said next: "Then I heard every creature in heaven and on earth and under the earth and on the sea, and all that is in them, singing."

Did you hear that? All of the creatures in heaven, and on the earth, and in the sea will be singing and praising Jesus! What kinds of creatures might there be in heaven? on the earth? under the earth? in the sea? And all of the creatures will be singing together! Won't that be wonderful?

When we get to heaven, we'll sing along with the whales and the birds and the gophers! Listen to what else the Bible says: "To him who sits on the throne and to the Lamb be praise and honor and glory and power, for ever and ever!" When we get to heaven, we'll be praising God and having a great time.

Right now, the choir is going to help us get an idea of what praising God in heaven might be like. Listen to their song. If you know the words, you can sing along. *Have the choir sit among the children, if possible, and sing a simple praise song such as "Alleluia" in harmony.*

That was beautiful singing. It makes me feel so good to sing praises. I don't think we'll miss our toys at all in heaven. There are too many other fun things to do there. Let's get a head start on praising God right now by saying a prayer.

♥ Dear God, thank you for making heaven such a fun place to be. We know we'll have fun singing and praising you. We want to spend our lives on earth praising you, too. Thank you for our homes here on earth, and thank you for preparing a home for us in heaven. In Jesus' name, amen. ♥

To help us all remember that in heaven we'll praise God with singing, I'm going to draw a musical note on each of your hands. Every time you look at it today, remember that we'll be singing to God in heaven. And remember to praise God here on earth, too! *Use washable marker to draw a musical note on the back of each child's hand.*

Theme:
Believing in Jesus is the way to heaven.

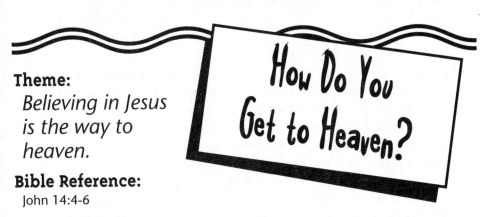

How Do You Get to Heaven?

Bible Reference:
John 14:4-6

Simple Supplies:
You'll need a Bible, paper, a basket, and markers or crayons. Before the message, draw a simple map of your church on a sheet of paper. Show how to get from the children's education area to the location where you and the children gather for the children's sermon.

Today we're going to talk a little bit about maps. Maps give us a way to write down directions on how to get from one place to another. Have you ever used a map to find out how to get somewhere? *Allow a few children to share their experiences. Then show the children your map.*

I've got a map here that I've drawn. Look carefully at the drawing. Can you tell what my map shows? *Help the children figure out that your map shows how to get from the children's education area of the church to the place where you gather for the children's sermon.*

That's right. I've drawn a map that shows how to get from the Sunday school area to right here, where we're gathered now. See the landmarks that I've drawn? They're clues from our church that could help us find our way.

It was easy for me to draw a map of our church. I've been in this building many times, and I know my way around. It would be much more difficult to draw a map of someplace I'd never been before. That's why it's always best to get directions from someone who's been where you're going.

Open your Bible to John 14:4-6. There was a time in the Bible when Jesus' followers needed directions. It was almost time for Jesus to go back to heaven. Jesus told his followers all about heaven and then he said, "You know the way to the place where I am going."

But the disciples were confused—they didn't understand what Jesus was saying. Thomas said, "We don't know where you are going, so how can we know the way?"

You see, Thomas and the others had never been to heaven—they didn't know how to get there.

But Jesus could give good directions because he'd been to heaven before. Jesus' directions are different from the directions you might be used to getting on a map or from other people. Listen to the directions that Jesus gave to his followers and that he gives to us. Jesus says, "I am the way and the truth and the life. No one comes to the Father except through me."

What do you suppose Jesus means by those directions? *Let children respond.* Thanks for those answers! Heaven isn't a place we can travel to in a car or on a plane. The only way we can get to heaven is by believing in Jesus. Jesus is our map and our key to heaven's door! Let's thank God for sending Jesus—our way to heaven!

♥ God, we thank you for sending Jesus to us. Help us to believe in him. Thank you for your love for us. In Jesus' name, amen. ♥

I've got some paper and crayons that I'd like to give you for a special assignment. I'd like each of you to draw a map that shows how to get to heaven. While you're drawing your map, remember what Jesus said—that he is the only way to heaven. So draw something that reminds you of Jesus. You might draw a picture of the cross to remind you of how Jesus died for us. Or you might draw a picture of a Christmas tree to remind you of Jesus' birth. Or you might draw a heart to remind you of how much Jesus loves us.

After the church service, when you're finished with your map, put your crayon in the basket that I've put in the back of the room. Then take your map and show it to someone here in church, and show them how they can get to heaven!

Distribute the paper and crayons, and send the children back to their seats.

Theme:
Heaven is a wonderful place where we can be with God.

Is Heaven Really in the Clouds?

Bible Reference:
Psalm 123:1

Simple Supplies:
You'll need a Bible, glow-in-the-dark star stickers, a flashlight, and an aluminum pie tin with holes poked in it. You'll also need someone to turn off the lights in your sanctuary if doing so will darken the room.

Have you ever gone outside at night to look at the stars? Let's pretend that it's a very dark night and we're outside looking at the stars. *Have your assistant darken the room. Shine the flashlight through the pie tin and project the "stars" onto the ceiling. If the ceiling is too far away, project the image on a nearby wall.*

Look at all those stars! They're so bright and twinkling. You know, some people think that heaven is beyond the stars. Sometimes when people are talking about the sky, they call it the heavens.

Where do you think heaven is? *Allow several children to respond.* The Bible doesn't tell us exactly where heaven is. But the Bible does talk about who is in heaven. God is in heaven! Listen to this verse from Psalm 123. *Open your Bible to Psalm 123:1, and show children the verse.* The Bible says, "I lift up my eyes to you, to you whose throne is in heaven." Heaven is where God is—it's God's home.

And when we believe in Jesus, someday we'll go to live with God in heaven. What do you think heaven looks like? What do you think heaven will sound like?

I'm so glad that Jesus came to give us a way to get to heaven. We may not know exactly where heaven is, I know it's a place I want to go!

Let's thank God for heaven. ❤ God, you've created everything—our beautiful world and the stars that shine brightly every night. God, we know that you've created heaven, too, and that if we believe in Jesus, we can live there with you someday. Thank you for giving us a way to live with you forever. Amen. ❤

I've brought a star sticker for each of you. Take your sticker home, and put it somewhere in your bedroom so you can see it at night. Every time you look at your star sticker, think about the home that you have in heaven because of Jesus. *Give each child a star sticker.*

Theme:

In heaven, we'll live with God as his children.

Bible Reference:

John 1:12

Simple Supplies:

You'll need a Bible; a baby animal, such as a bunny, a puppy, or a kitten; and dog biscuits. If you don't have access to a baby animal, borrow some stuffed animal toys from the church nursery.

I have a very special guest to introduce to you today during our talk. But this guest is a little bit shy, so I need you all to be on your best behavior. Everyone will get a chance to meet this very important guest, so please remember to wait your turn. We don't want to crowd around our guest and scare him. Are you ready to meet him?

Bring out the baby animal you've brought, and give the children each a chance to pet it. Tell the children what the animal's name is and who its owner is. You may want to have the owner share a little information about the pet.

I've been wondering a little bit about this animal. What do you think this animal's mom and dad look like? What do you think this animal will look like when it's all grown up? Do you think there's any chance that this puppy might grow up to be a cat or an elephant?

That was kind of a silly question. We know that kittens grow up to be cats. They won't turn into parrots or monkeys. The same thing is true for dogs and for all other animals. And the same thing is true for you, too. When you grow up, you'll be an adult person like your mom and dad. But no matter how old you get, your mom and dad will still be your mom and dad, won't they?

Open your Bible to John 1:12. Some people think that when people go to heaven they'll be angels. But God's Word says that's not the case. Listen to what the Bible says, and listen for what we'll be. In the book of John the Bible says, "Yet to all who received him, to those who believed in [Jesus'] name, he gave the right to become children of God."

Did you hear what the Bible says? What will we be in heaven? *Help the children discuss and discover that in heaven they'll be God's children, not angels.*

That's right. God loves us so much that when we believe in Jesus, we become God's children. And we'll always be God's children, even when we get to heaven. When we go to heaven we'll be there as God's children, not as angels. Isn't it great to know that God loves us that much? Let's thank him right now for making us his children.

♥ God, we thank you today because you are our father and you've given us the right to become your children if we believe in Jesus. Thank you for loving us, and thank you for preparing a wonderful home where we can live with you forever as your children. Amen. ♥

I've got something unusual for you to take home with you today. It's a treat to eat, but it's not something that people usually eat.

Today I've brought each of you a puppy biscuit. Take home this puppy biscuit and feed it to your dog or give it to a neighbor to feed to their dog. Then remember that just as a puppy won't turn into a cat, you won't turn into an angel when you go to heaven. You're God's child and you always will be! *Hand out the dog biscuits.*

Theme:
Jesus is all we need to get to heaven.

Bible Reference:
John 3:16

Simple Supplies:
You'll need a Bible and elf sandwich cookies.

I'd like to tell you a story about Kirby the basketball player. This isn't a true story—it's only make-believe.

Have you ever noticed how basketball players are usually tall people? Well, Kirby was the tallest kid in school. Everyone said, "Have you seen how tall Kirby is? He's going to be a great basketball player!"

When it was time for the basketball team to practice, all the other players worked on their dribbling. Let's pretend to dribble. *Have the children pretend to dribble basketballs.*

All of the players also practiced their shooting and passing. Let's all pretend to shoot a basketball out into the congregation and see if the grown-ups will pass the balls back to us. *Have the children pretend to throw balls out to the congregation, and wait to see if the congregation pretends to throw them back.*

But Kirby said, "I'm already the tallest person in school, what do I need to practice for?" So Kirby only went to practice once in a while, and he never worked very hard on his basketball skills. While all the other kids practiced, Kirby just talked about how great it was to be tall.

Soon it was time to play the first game of the season. The team put on their uniforms, and they ran out onto the court to play. Kirby looked very fine in his uniform. He stood up tall and proud—after all, he was the tallest person there. How do you think Kirby did in that game? *Allow the children to respond.*

That's right. Kirby had trouble dribbling the ball. He had never really learned how to pass the ball to his teammates, and every time he shot the ball it bounced off the backboard without making a score.

Kirby learned a lesson in that game. What do you think he learned? *Allow the children to respond.* Kirby learned that being tall isn't the most important thing about being a good basketball player. Being tall helps, but you've got to work on your skills, too.

There are lots of times when people get confused about what's most important. We know that it's important to do good things for other people.

What are some of the good things we can do for others?

It isn't a bad thing to try hard to do good things for other people. God wants us to do good things. But sometimes people think that if they do enough good things, they'll go to heaven. But just as being tall isn't the most important thing about being a good basketball player, being good isn't the most important thing when it comes to going to heaven.

God knew that no matter how many good things we did, we'd never be good enough to go to heaven. That's why God sent Jesus. To go to heaven, all we need to do is believe in Jesus.

That's what the Bible says in John 3:16. *Open your Bible to the verse.* If you know the verse, go ahead and say it with me. "For God so loved the world that he gave his one and only Son, that whoever believes in him shall not perish but have eternal life."

We know that Jesus is all we need to get to heaven. Let's thank God for giving us Jesus.

♥ Dear God, we thank you that we don't have to be perfect to go to heaven. We know that if we believe in Jesus, someday we'll live in heaven with you. Thank you for giving us a way to get to heaven. In Jesus' name, amen. ♥

Today I've brought a special treat to help you remember the story. Remember how Kirby thought he had to be tall to be a good basketball player? Well, I've brought little elf cookies to help us all remember that being tall isn't the most important thing about being a basketball player. As you eat your cookie, remember that being good isn't the most important thing about getting to heaven—believing in Jesus is! *Hand out the elf sandwich cookies.*

Theme:

Angels praise and serve God, and they help people, too.

Do Angels Go to Church?

Bible Reference:

Psalm 103:20 (NCV); Hebrews 1:14 (NCV)

Simple Supplies:

You'll need a Bible, angel ornaments, napkins, and angel food cake torn into bite-sized pieces.

Today we're going to talk about angels. I've brought some angel figures for you to look at. These are angels that I have at my house. *Pass around the angel ornaments.*

It's kind of funny that we decorate our houses with angels only at Christmastime. There are many stories in the Bible other than the Christmas story that have angels in them. Let's put our heads together and see if we can think of any of those stories. Can you remember any Bible stories that have angels in them? *Help children think of angel stories from the Bible. You might need to prompt them with hints about Mary, the shepherds, the empty tomb, Abraham, Paul in jail, and so on.*

What did the angels do in those stories—what was the angel's job in each of these stories? *Allow the children to respond.*

There are many angels in the Bible, but it's still hard to have a good understanding of just what angels do and even what they look like. I don't know if angels sleep at night, or if they eat or play games. And I don't know if angels go to church.

But I did find a verse in the Bible that tells us a little bit about what angels do. *Open your Bible to Psalm 103:20, and show children the verse.* It's Psalm 103:20 and it says, "You who are his angels, praise the Lord. You are the mighty warriors who do what he says and who obey his voice."

There's a lot in that verse for angels to do. Let's go back through the verse slowly. I'll read the verse again, and you listen and be ready to tell me what you've learned about angels. Ready? Here it is. "You who are his angels, praise the Lord. You are the mighty warriors who do what he says and who obey his voice."

What do angels do? *Allow the children to respond.* It sounds as if angels do whatever God wants them to do. Angels praise God, do what God says, and obey God's voice.

Let's stand up and play a game about what angels do. All of you pretend to be angels. We'll play this game like Simon Says only instead of saying "Simon Says," I'll say, "God told the angels to..." Then I'll finish the sentence with what I want you to do. Ready? Here we go.

God told the angels to

- say, "Praise the Lord!"
- tell someone that Jesus loves them.
- hop on one foot.
- say, "Be not afraid."
- make muscles as if you're a mighty warrior.
- take a seat.

Whew! Angels must be busy doing God's work all over the world!

You know, in some ways angels are a lot like us—they're supposed to obey God no matter what. I found another verse that tells us something else that angels do. *Open your Bible to Hebrews 1:14, and show children the verse.*

The verse is Hebrews 1:14 and it says, "All the angels are spirits who serve God and are sent to help those who will receive salvation." Who do you think the verse is talking about— who are the angels supposed to help?

That's right. Angels are busy helping us. How do you think angels help people? Has an angel ever helped you or someone you know?

It's good to hear your stories about angels. But even if you didn't have a story, you can know that angels are helping you even when you can't see them. Let's thank God for sending angels to help us.

♥ God, we know that you love us and you want to protect us and keep us safe. Thank you so much for your promise to send angels to help us. We know they're all around us. Amen. ♥

All this talk about angels has made me hungry! How would you all like some angel food cake? Here's a napkin for each of you. *Give each child a napkin.*

Now I'm going to give each of you two small pieces of cake. You can eat one piece yourself. But as you head back to your seat, give the other piece to someone else in the congregation, and tell them that angels obey God and protect people.

Pass out the cake, and send the children back to their seats.

Theme:
God is preparing a special place for us.

Bible Reference:
John 14:2

What Will My Room Look Like in Heaven?

Simple Supplies:
You'll need a Bible, yellow paper plates, gumdrops, and marshmallows.

Bedrooms are special places, aren't they? People usually keep some of their special belongings in their bedrooms—things like their toys and their clothes and their stuffed animals. And people spend a lot of time in their beds sleeping and having good dreams.

Yes, bedrooms are special. What's your favorite thing about your bedroom at home?

Someday we're going to have a bedroom in heaven. Jesus is already up in heaven getting it all ready for us. This is what he told his disciples in the book of John. *Open your Bible to John 14:2.* Here's what Jesus says. "In my Father's house are many rooms; if it were not so, I would have told you. I am going there to prepare a place for you."

Wow! There's a place just for you up in heaven! What do you suppose your room in heaven is like?

I've brought some things to help us think a little bit about what our rooms in heaven might be like. *Bring out the gumdrops, paper plates, and marshmallows.* The Bible talks about heaven having streets of gold. So I've brought gold-colored paper plates to remind us of the golden streets. *Give each child a paper plate.*

The Bible also says that the gates to heaven are like big pearls. Pearls are white, so I've brought marshmallows to be the gates. *Give each child several marshmallows, but ask them not to eat them yet.*

The Bible also says that heaven is full of precious stones like rubies, sapphires, emeralds, and diamonds. I've brought some gumdrops to remind us of the precious stones. *Give each child several gumdrops.*

Let's use these treats to build what our heavenly bedrooms might look like. Arrange the treats on your plates of gold in ways that make you think of what your room in heaven might look like.

Give the children a few moments to build rooms by stacking and arranging the snack items. Then let the kids tell you about the rooms they've built.

Your rooms all look so special. And heaven really is a wonderful place! I'm so glad that Jesus loves us so much that he's getting heaven ready for us.

It'll probably be a long, long time before any of you will get to use your rooms in heaven. But God is making sure that your room will be ready when you get to heaven. In the meantime, God takes care of us while we live here, too, in our regular bedrooms. Let's thank God for his love and care.

♥ God, you've created everything we see, but you still care about what happens to us every day. You love us so much that you're preparing a place for us in heaven. Thank you for taking care of us and thank you for loving us. Amen. ♥ *Have the children take home their gumdrop rooms.*

Theme:
Angels appear in different ways.

Bible Reference:
Psalm 91:11

Simple Supplies:
You'll need a Bible, paper, and crayons.

Today, we're going to draw some pictures. I'm going to hand out paper and crayons, and I'd like each of you to draw a picture of an angel. *Hand out the paper and crayons.*

While you're working on your pictures, why don't you tell me what you know about angels. *Have the children tell you about angels. If they have trouble getting started, ask questions such as "What Bible stories have angels in them?" "What do angels do?" "Where do angels live?" and "What do angels look like?" When the children are finished drawing, have them hold up their pictures for everyone to see.*

There's something very interesting about every angel picture I've ever seen. Whenever we draw angels, we give them wings. Otherwise they'd look like people. But did you know that in the Bible, angels don't usually have wings?

There's a story in the book of Genesis—the very first book of the Bible—about a time when visitors came to give a message to Abraham. The visitors looked just like regular people, but they were angels. The angels came to tell Abraham that he and his wife, Sarah, were going to have a baby even though they were old enough to be grandparents. And sure enough; it happened just the way the angels said it would.

Angels are mysterious creatures. We don't know exactly what they look like. But the Bible does tell us some things about angels. *Open your Bible to Psalm 91:11.* The Bible says in Psalm 91:11 that God "will command his angels concerning you to guard you in all your ways." So that means that angels are in charge of guarding us and protecting us!

To help us understand how angels protect us, let's pretend that these angel drawings are real angels sent by God for our protection. Let's put the angels in a circle surrounding us. We'll stay here in the middle where we're all safe. *Give the children a moment to arrange their angel drawings in a circle behind them.*

Now let's thank God for giving us angels to protect us. ❤ God, we thank you for creating angels to bring us messages and to guard us. We feel safe knowing that your angels are protecting us. Thank you for loving us. Amen. ❤ *Have the children take home their angel drawings.*

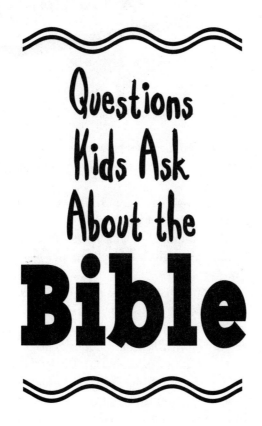

Questions
Kids Ask
About the
Bible

Theme:
Jesus wants us to teach his truth to others.

Bible Reference:
Matthew 28:18-20

Simple Supplies:
You'll need a Bible and a feather for each child.

Do you have any ideas about what this feather could have to do with our Christian lives? *Let kids come up with lots of ideas, and affirm each contribution.*

Well, this is what I think. When I saw this feather, it reminded me of a bird. When I thought about a bird, I was reminded of freedom. When I thought about freedom, I remembered that Jesus came to set us free. When I thought about being free, I thought about all the people who don't know what Jesus came to do.

Then I thought, "If I could just get this feather out to people, the whole world would know about Jesus..." How do you think that idea will work? *Kids might answer that it's just a feather and no one's going to know what you're thinking, or that there's only one feather but millions of people in the world.*

The idea of telling the whole world about Jesus is good, though, right? In fact, it comes directly from the Bible. *Open your Bible to Matthew 28:18-20, and show children the passage.* Listen to what the Bible says in the book of Matthew: "Then Jesus came to them and said, 'All authority in heaven and on earth has been given to me. Therefore go and make disciples of all nations, baptizing them in the name of the Father and of the Son and of the Holy Spirit, and teaching them to obey everything I have commanded you. And surely I am with you always, to the very end of the age.' "

I just love that passage! I love knowing what Jesus wants us to do, and I love knowing that Jesus will always be with us. What does it mean to make a disciple of someone?

That's right. It means to teach that person to love and follow Jesus. What are some of your ideas about how we can make disciples of all nations?

Good ideas! I think the things you said were exactly some of the things that Jesus had in mind when he chose the twelve disciples. And I think we can use our feather to get an idea of how telling about Jesus works.

Let's imagine that this feather is carrying the good news about Jesus. I want this message to get to the ends of the earth. Let's pretend that all the area between us and the back wall of this room is like the distance between us and the ends of the earth.

The message about Jesus needs to reach the people in the back row. *Stand still and throw the feather with gusto. Make several attempts.*

Wait, this isn't working. How can I get this feather to the back row? *Let children offer suggestions.* Yes, carrying it would work to get the message to the ends of the earth, over there in the back row.

Jesus told his disciples that the message would need to be carried not only to all nations, but also to the end of the age. That means over time. Now I could carry this feather over distance, but I can't travel through time to get this message to people who live in the future. Neither could the disciples who first heard Jesus' words. So how did the disciples get the message from their time to our time? *Give children a chance to respond.*

Good ideas. To show you how it might have worked, we need to make a straight line from here all the way to the back row. *Give the kids time to regroup so that they form a long line.*

Now we'll pretend that those of us who are at the very front of this line by me live in Bible time. And those of you at the very back of the line live sometime in the future. Now remember, the feather represents the good news about Jesus.

I'll give the feather to the first person in line. You give it to the next person. When the feather comes to you, pass it on to the next person. If it drops, just pick it up and continue passing it to the next person.

After the feather has been passed down the line, congratulate each child for doing his or her part, then have the kids hold hands. Have the ends of the line walk toward each other until the line becomes a circle in the center of the room.

Just as we're joined together here in this room, we're also joined together with all the people who have followed Jesus' command throughout history. We're part of a very important group of people—God's messengers of the good news about Jesus! The Christians who went before us did a good job—that's how we know about Jesus today. Now it's our turn to tell others about Jesus, so everyone can learn the good news!

Let's pray together that God will help us do the job as well as we did when we were practicing with the feather.

❤ Dear God, you put a great plan into practice with the twelve disciples who walked with Jesus. Now you're trusting us to keep carrying the message of your love to others. Help us to be faithful as we tell others about you. Amen. ❤

Give each child a feather. Take this feather home to use as a bookmark at Matthew 28 in your own Bibles, where Jesus tells us to go and make disciples of all nations.

Theme:

God gives us the abilities to do the jobs he has for us.

Bible Reference:
Philippians 4:13

Simple Supplies:
You'll need a Bible, pictures of animals (including some little-known, challenging ones), and animal crackers.

How Did Adam Think of All the Names for the Animals?

Most of us have chores, or jobs, that we do at home. What are some chores that you do at home? When God put Adam on the earth, he gave him chores to do. One of those chores was to name the animals. We don't use the exact same names that Adam chose because his language was different from ours, but our names for the animals come from the names he chose. Let's see if we know these animals. *Hold up the animal pictures, and have children name the animals.*

What do you think are some of the problems you might have faced if you were in charge of naming each animal? It might have been difficult, but God gave Adam the help he needed to name the animals. Can you tell about a job that you felt was too difficult for you? How did God help you?

Open your Bible to Philippians 4:13. In the book of Philippians, the Bible talks about doing tough jobs. Listen: "I can do everything through him who gives me strength." God had chores for Adam to do, and God has chores for us to do, too. And this Scripture tells us that God will help us with anything we have to do.

God doesn't need us to rename the animals, even though it might be kind of fun. What are things God does ask us to do? *Let children respond.* We know that God gives us the strength to do the things he asks, just as he helped Adam with naming the animals.

Pass some animal crackers to each child. As we're enjoying our animal crackers, let's give our cracker animals new names, just for fun. Share your new names with a partner, then we'll pray together.

Allow a moment for kids to name and eat their animal crackers. That was fun! Now let's have fun talking to God. ❤ Dear God, thank you for using people to do your work on earth. Help us remember that you give us strength to do whatever you ask. Amen. ❤

Theme:
God watches over us wherever we are.

Bible Reference:
Psalm 121:5-8

How Could Jonah Live in the Belly of a Fish?

Simple Supplies:
You'll need a Bible; a can of mackerel, sardines, or other strong-smelling fish, emptied into an airtight plastic container; a spray bottle of water; and enough fish crackers for all the children to have some.

How many of you have ever caught a fish? What was that like? Do you remember the story in the Bible of how Jonah was swallowed by a big fish? I want to give you some idea of what it must have been like for Jonah when he was inside the belly of that giant fish.

First, everyone close your eyes, because it was dark in the fish's belly. I'm going to walk among you with something to smell. Keep your eyes closed until I tell you to open them. *Open the container of fish, and walk around so kids can smell the contents.*

Without opening your eyes, tell me what you think you smelled. Right! Yucky fish! And it sure could have smelled like that in the big fish's belly, because big fish eat little fish. Now you can open your eyes.

As the kids open their eyes, spray some water from the spray bottle over their heads so that it falls onto them. It was probably a little wet in there, too. What other things do you think Jonah might have experienced inside the big fish?

Whatever it was like, it sure wasn't a good place to be! Jonah wound up in the belly of a fish because he was trying to run away from what God wanted him to do. Have you ever tried to run away from God? How did you feel? Do you think anyone can ever really hide from God? *Give children a chance to respond to your questions.*

Could God see Jonah in the belly of that fish? God certainly took care of Jonah, even inside that fish! Jonah was in a bad situation, but he was never really alone, was he? We know that God took care of Jonah, because Jonah went on to preach at Nineveh after the fish spit him out.

Open your Bible to Psalm 121:5-8. The book of Psalms tells us how God takes care of us. Listen. "The Lord watches over you—the Lord is your shade at your right hand; the sun will not harm you by day, nor the moon by night.

The Lord will keep you from all harm—he will watch over your life; the Lord will watch over your coming and going both now and forevermore."

Wow! God is always taking care of us! God took care of Jonah, even in a fish's belly. And God will take care of us, too, no matter where we are or how we got there.

Let's thank God for taking care of us. ❤ Dear God, thank you for always caring about us and for always taking care of us. Help us to always follow you. In Jesus' name, amen. ❤

A big fish swallowed Jonah. Here are some little fish that you can swallow! *Give each child a few fish crackers.* As you go back to your seats and eat your fish crackers, remember: God will always care for you, just as he cared for Jonah.

Theme:
God wants us to obey him.

Bible Reference:
Luke 11:28

Simple Supplies:
You'll need a Bible, a
"treasure map" (a paper with simple
directions as described in the sermon), and candy. Before
the meeting, give all the candy to an adult in the congregation, and ask this
person to sit in the front row.

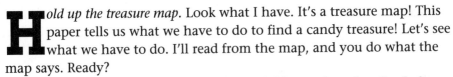

Hold up the treasure map. Look what I have. It's a treasure map! This
paper tells us what we have to do to find a candy treasure! Let's see
what we have to do. I'll read from the map, and you do what the
map says. Ready?

*Read from the paper, and wait for all the children to do each action before
reading the next one.* Hop on one foot. Shake the hand of an adult. Say hello
to someone wearing green. Gather around (name of person with candy). *Help
this person distribute the candy to the children, then have kids sit down again.*

Why do you think you had to go through so many steps to get the
candy? Do you ever have to follow directions in real life to get something
you want? What about following directions to make something good? Do
you have to follow directions to make cookies? to make a model car? to put
together a new toy?

When we follow or obey directions, good things often happen, don't
they? When we obeyed the directions of our treasure map, we got yummy
candy. And when we follow the directions on a recipe, the result is good
cookies or food. When we obey the directions to put together a new toy, we
get something fun to play with.

In the same way, God asks us to obey him and follow his directions.
Sometimes this can be hard. What are some of the directions that God gives
us? When is it hard for you to follow God's directions?

Thank you for those answers! You know, in Bible times people offered
animal sacrifices to God. That means that they killed the animals; they
offered the lives of the animals to show that they loved God and were
willing to obey him. The Bible tells about a man named Abraham who had
only one child, a son named Isaac. God asked Abraham to sacrifice Isaac's
life to God. This would have been very hard for Abraham to do. But

Abraham was prepared to obey God.

He gathered the supplies he would need and took Isaac to a place to be sacrificed. But before he could complete the job, God told Abraham not to sacrifice Isaac after all. God wanted to see if Abraham would obey something very, very hard to do. And when God saw that Abraham would obey, he let him keep his son and rewarded Abraham with even more children!

Open your Bible to Luke 11:28. God's Word reminds us that God wants us to obey him, too. In Luke 11:28, Jesus says, "Blessed...are those who hear the word of God and obey it." This means God blesses us for obeying the Bible. The Bible is kind of like our own treasure map. When we follow the directions that God gives us in the Bible, God blesses us. Let's thank God for caring about us so much.

❤ Dear God, help us to obey you and always follow your directions, even when it seems hard. Thank you for blessing us and loving us. In Jesus' name, amen. ❤

Theme:
God wants us to be faithful.

Bible Reference:
1 Corinthians 10:13b

Simple Supplies:
You'll need a Bible and cookies. You may want to prep the "punished" child before the meeting so he or she understands the activity and isn't embarrassed.

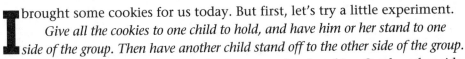

Why Did Peter Say He Didn't Know Jesus?

I brought some cookies for us today. But first, let's try a little experiment. *Give all the cookies to one child to hold, and have him or her stand to one side of the group. Then have another child stand off to the other side of the group.* On one side of me is (name) with a large supply of cookies. On the other side of me is (name) who doesn't have any cookies. In fact, not only does (name) not have any cookies, let's pretend he (or she) broke a window with a baseball and is about to be punished! Now I want all of you to think about who you'd rather play with right now. Go and stand beside the child you'd rather play with.

After children make their choices, have them sit where they are. Why did you choose the person with cookies? Why did you choose the person who's about to be punished? Have people ever treated you as if they didn't like you?

Jesus understands what this is like. One of his closest friends was named Peter. When Peter saw Jesus doing miracles and causing a big stir among people, Peter was glad to be Jesus' friend. But things changed.

Suddenly Jesus was arrested and beaten. Jesus was about to be killed, and the soldiers were looking for the friends of Jesus, too. Peter changed his mind then! He was so afraid that he told people he didn't even know who Jesus was!

But later, when Peter realized what he'd done, he was very sorry. Jesus understood and forgave Peter. Peter later became a strong leader of Christians.

God wants us to be faithful. What do you think that means? Being faithful means that God wants us to stick with our friends, our family, and especially with God, even when it seems hard. *Open your Bible to 1 Corinthians 10:13b.* In fact, the Bible tells us that "God is faithful; he will not let you be tempted beyond what you can bear." This means that God will help us do what's right even when it's hard. We can always count on God.

Have both children used in your activity help pass out cookies to everyone. Before you take these cookies back to your seat, let's pray to God. ♥ Dear God, thank you for being faithful to us. Help us to be faithful to you. Amen. ♥

Theme:
God can do amazing things!

Bible Reference:
Matthew 19:26

Simple Supplies:
You'll need a Bible; a live, tame animal; and animal stickers.

Did Balaam's Donkey Really Talk?

Show the animal to the children. If the animal is trained to respond to commands, demonstrate these to the children.

Do you think this animal can talk to us? Have you ever heard an animal talk? You've probably heard a cat "meow," a bird "chirp," or a dog "bark." Some birds can even be trained to copy our voices, but the bird isn't really telling us its thoughts; it's just copying.

The Bible tells us about an animal that really talked out loud in words a human could understand! Have you ever heard about Balaam and his donkey? Balaam was trying to do something wrong, and God made Balaam's donkey speak to him to get Balaam's attention. What do you think Balaam thought when he heard his donkey talking?

I've never heard of any other time when God made an animal talk. But I have heard of other amazing things God has done. Can you think of any Bible stories where something amazing happened? *Help children remember miracles such as Creation, parting of the Red Sea, or Jesus raising someone from the dead.*

What about times God has answered your prayers or taken care of you in an amazing way? *Allow several children to share.*

Open your Bible to Matthew 19:26. The Bible tells us that we can expect God to do amazing things. Matthew 19:26 says, "Jesus looked at them and said, 'With man this is impossible, but with God all things are possible.' " We probably won't ever hear a donkey talk, but we know that anything's possible with God in control!

Give each child an animal sticker. Take this animal sticker home as a reminder that God can do amazing things! Now let's pray.

❤ Dear God, thank you for all the amazing things you do each day. Thank you for making the sun come up, for making flowers grow, and for showing us your love. You are amazing! Amen. ❤

Theme:
God wants us to get along with others.

Bible Reference:
Ephesians 4:32

Simple Supplies:
You'll need a Bible, five to ten pictures of people in different occupations (such as firefighter, garbage collector, nurse, or teacher) mounted on 8×11-inch pieces of cardboard, and inexpensive friendship bracelets.

Do you ever fight with your brothers or sisters? How about with your friends? What do you fight about?

Did you know that even Jesus' disciples argued with each other? What do you think they fought about? The disciples argued about who was the most important! Let's try to figure out what people are the most important.

Show children the pictures of people in different occupations. Let's set these pictures in the order of which ones are most important. *Allow time for discussion, moving the pictures around as children offer suggestions. After several minutes, stop and point out problems with the rankings. Use the following suggestions.*

Are garbage collectors really so far down on the list? Without garbage collectors, we'd get sick from the bugs and the smell. How can doctors be more important than teachers? Don't doctors have to go to school too?

Allow more discussion and moving around of the pictures. Then stop the discussion. Can you see how the disciples might argue about who was more important? We can't seem to agree, either! But Jesus has an important message for us.

Open your Bible to Ephesians 4:32. Ephesians 4:32 tells us how we should treat each other. The verse says, "Be kind and compassionate to one another, forgiving each other, just as in Christ God forgave you."

What are ways we can show kindness to others? God wants us to get along with others, not argue with them! Let's thank God for teaching us how to get along with our families and friends.

❤ Dear God, thank you for teaching us to be kind to others. Help us to get along with others, instead of worrying about who's more important. In Jesus' name, amen. ❤

I have a friendship bracelet for each of you today. Wear your bracelet to remind you that God wants us to get along with each other. *Give each child a friendship bracelet.*

75

Theme:
God answers our prayers.

Bible Reference:
1 Kings 3:12

How Did Solomon Get So Smart?

Simple Supplies:

You'll need a Bible, a cordless phone (or phone on an extension cord), and cookies. Arrange ahead of time to call your church custodian or a pastor during the message.

I brought some cookies for us to enjoy today! But I think we'd better ask permission before we eat the cookies in this room. Who should we call? *Let children offer suggestions.* I think we should call (name), our church custodian, to make sure it's OK to get a few crumbs on the carpet.

Bring out your phone. Does anyone know the phone number? What should we do if I get a busy signal? What should we do if I get an answering machine? *Give children time to respond.* Oh, I have the number here. I'll dial. Here goes.

Dial the phone, and wait for the custodian to answer as arranged. Ask for permission to eat the cookies, then hang up.

He said "yes!" We can have the cookies! All I had to do was to let him (or her) know what we needed, and he (or she) gave us the answer right away.

Before I pass out the cookies though, I have a question. I wonder, do you ever call God on the phone? How does God know what we need or what we want to thank him for?

When we pray, we're talking to God. We can go to God in prayer with all of our questions and needs. What does God do when lots of people talk to him at once? Does God ever need an answering machine? Why or why not? *Let children answer.*

You're right! God is so powerful, he can listen to everyone's prayers at once! And God always answers our prayers! Just as when we called to ask permission to eat the cookies, and the custodian answered the phone, God always answers us.

Even though we're all glad the custodian said "yes," he (or she) might have said "no" to us or "wait until after church." And it's the same with God. He can tell us yes, or no, or wait until later. But he always, always answers us.

The Bible tells us about a man named Solomon who asked God for something. Solomon asked God to give him wisdom. He wanted to be a good king, so he asked God to help him make good decisions by being wise and smart.

Open your Bible to 1 Kings 3:12. The Bible tells us in 1 Kings 3:12 how

God answered Solomon. "I will do what you have asked. I will give you a wise and discerning heart." God answered "yes" to Solomon. God answered Solomon's prayer, and gave him lots of wisdom. Solomon is now remembered for being very, very wise. God answered his prayer!

What kinds of things do you ask God to help you with? How has God answered your prayers? God answered Solomon's prayer and gave him wisdom. And God answers our prayers, too. Let's pray.

❤ Dear God, thank you for listening to our prayers and always answering them. Even when you say no, or wait until later, we know you've heard us and answered us. Thank you for these cookies. Amen. ❤

Wait! I almost forgot! We're allowed to eat our cookies. As you eat your cookie, remember that God always answers our prayers, just as he did for Solomon. *Give each child a cookie to take along.*

Theme:

The Ten Commandments help us follow God.

Why Does God Have So Many Rules?

Bible Reference:

Exodus 20:1-17

Simple Supplies:

You'll need a Bible, markers, scissors, construction paper, tape, and colored dot stickers.

Before the sermon, write the numbers 1 through 10 in large print on separate sheets of construction paper. On another sheet of paper, write "home" in large print. Create an obstacle course by taping the papers to the floor, in a random pattern, but close enough together so children can step from one numbered-paper to another. Have the obstacle course end at "home."

Also, count out ten colored dot stickers for each child, and number the stickers 1 through 10 with a marker. Place all the "1" stickers near the "1" paper on the obstacle course. Place all the "2" stickers near the "2" paper, and so on. Finally, cut a 1×10-inch strip of construction paper for each child.

Today we're going to talk about rules. Who can name some of the rules you have to follow at home or at school? All of us have to follow a lot of rules, even though sometimes we may not want to.

But the rules God made for us are to help us as we move closer to him. And the Ten Commandments are special rules to help us show our love for God and for one another. So let's make sure we know what those Commandments are!

Let's count the Ten Commandments on our fingers. *Open your Bible to Exodus 20:1-17, and show the children where the Ten Commandments are. Say aloud the following simplified version of the Commandments. Allow children time to repeat each Commandment after you've said it.*

1. Don't worship other gods.
2. Don't have idols.
3. Don't misuse God's name.
4. Keep the Sabbath day holy.
5. Honor your mom and dad.
6. Don't kill.
7. Be true to your husband or wife.

8. Don't steal.

9. Don't lie about others.

10. Don't wish you had what others have.

Good job! Now that we know what the Ten Commandments are, let's see how they can help us follow God.

Tape a strip of paper around each child's wrist. These Top Ten Bands will help you to remember the Ten Commandments as you go on a fun obstacle course. You're going to step on each number, making sure you don't touch the ground, and try to make it all the way to "home." *Point out where "home" is.*

As you stop at each number, take a sticker and stick it on your Top Ten Band. But watch out—there are traps out there that will try to keep you from getting home. Be careful! Ready? Let's go!

Lead a group of six or seven kids through the obstacle course, making sure each child stops to stick a sticker on his or her Top Ten Band at each number. If you have more than six or seven children, have adult volunteers lead other small groups of children through the course.

As children move along, shout out comments such as, "Careful, don't step on that pile of lies!" or "Oh, no—some people over there want you to steal; don't listen to them!" Allow all the children to travel through the obstacle course. Then have kids sit down.

Great job! It's a good thing we had those numbers to walk on to help us get safely home. You know, those numbers are like the Ten Commandments. God's rules help us travel safely on our way through life. And now, we have these colorful Top Ten Bands to show that the Ten Commandments help us follow God.

Have kids hold up their bands as you close in prayer.

❤ Dear God, thank you for giving us the Ten Commandments to help keep us safe as we find our home with you. Help us to use our Top Ten Bands as reminders of how we can walk closer to you, step by step, every single day. In Jesus' name, amen. ❤

Questions
Kids Ask
About
Life

Theme:
God gave us
parents to love
and watch over
us.

Bible Reference:
Ephesians 6:1-3

Simple Supplies:
You'll need a Bible and a construction paper heart with an X cut in the center for every child.

Today we're going to talk about parents. To understand why God gave us parents, let's play a game. *Have the children form two equal groups, the Parents and the Children. Then have the two groups stand back-to-back. Tell kids to stay standing back-to-back and not to look behind them.*

Stand in front of the Parents. OK Parents, look at me and do what I do. *Show Parents how to make a large imaginary stitch several times, and lead them in the action.* Great! Children, now do the same action. What's the matter? Why can't you do the same motion the Parents just did? That's right! You need someone to show you what to do. You need a model!

Parents, stand in front of the Children. Now show them the action. Now let's do the action together. Congratulations! Shake hands with the person in front of you, then sit down.

It was an easy action to follow, once someone showed you how to do it. That's one of the reasons God gave parents to children—to show them how to do things. *Open your Bible to Ephesians 6:1-3.* Listen to the plan for families that God gives us in Ephesians 6:1-3. "Children, obey your parents in the Lord, for this is right. 'Honor your father and mother'—which is the first commandment with a promise—'that it may go well with you and that you may enjoy long life on the earth.' "

Honoring our fathers and mothers by doing what they teach us helps us to learn about God. What have your parents taught you about God?

What can you do to honor your parents?

I'm going to give each of you a paper heart that you can wear over a button or through a shoelace. You even might like to give the heart to one of your parents today to show how you love and honor them.

Give each child a paper heart. Now let's pray to our heavenly parent. 💜 Dear God, thank you for giving us parents to show us how to live. Help us to honor them by obeying them, just as you planned. In Jesus' name, amen. 💜

Theme:
God reveals his plans for us.

Bible Reference:
James 1:5

Simple Supplies:
You'll need a Bible and small, polished stones that can be concealed in your hand.

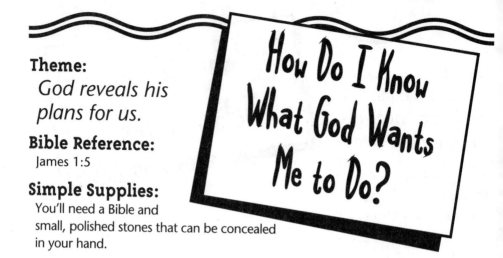

How Do I Know What God Wants Me to Do?

Conceal a stone in one hand before you begin to speak. Let's play a guessing game today. *Hold out both fists.* I have something in one of my hands. Can you guess which one? *Play the game a few times, putting your hands behind your back to conceal your movements.*

In this game, you tried to guess which hand the stone was in. Playing a guessing game is OK for fun, but not for the important parts of life, such as what God wants us to do. We can't base those choices on guesses.

Hold out the stone in one hand for kids to see. We need to know what God wants us to do. Can you tell about a time when you needed to figure out what God wanted you to do? What did you do to find out?

God never plays a guessing game with us or tries to make us guess the wrong answer. *Open your Bible to James 1:5.* The book of James talks about how we can know what God wants. Listen. "If any of you lacks wisdom, he should ask God, who gives generously to all without finding fault, and it will be given to him."

This verse tells us that if we need to know something, we can ask God. It also says that God will be generous when he gives us answers. What does "generous" mean? *Let children offer answers.*

That's right. When someone is generous, they give and give and give. How does God give us wisdom? *Kids might answer that God gives wisdom through the Bible, prayer, or other Christians.*

Thanks for your answers! God doesn't play games with his wisdom. He promises to give it to us freely. *Give each child a polished stone.* God's wisdom is yours for the asking—no guessing required! Hold your shiny stone firmly in your hand as we thank God for his rock-solid promise.

♥ Dear God, thank you for promising to give us your wisdom. Help us make wise choices that please you. Help us listen to you and obey you. In Jesus' name, amen. ♥

Theme:
We go to church to learn, praise, and grow.

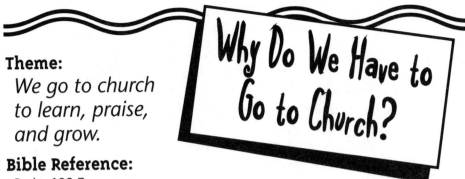

Why Do We Have to Go to Church?

Bible Reference:
Psalm 132:7

Simple Supplies:
You'll need a Bible, a simple construction paper hand cutout for each child, and a pair of white gloves (optional). Use the "Happy Hand" handout on page 84 as a guide for your paper hand cutouts.

What are some things that you do when you come to church? Why do we come to church?

God wants us to come to church. He wants us to be together as his people. He wants us to learn how to follow him and obey him. *Open your Bible to Psalm 132:7 and read the verse:* "Let us go to his dwelling place; let us worship at his footstool." This verse was sung by the Israelites as they went to the temple to worship God. They wanted to worship at God's footstool, or his feet.

What are some reasons we go to church each week? *Let children respond. Begin to put on the white gloves for effect.* I'm going to teach you how to say three reasons with your hands by using sign language.

Guess which reason this is. *Lay your left hand out in front of you, palm up. Move your right hand so it looks as if you are picking up something from your left hand and placing it on your forehead.*

Can you guess what this sign means? It means to learn. We come to church to learn. Now you try it. *Repeat the sign until all the children can do it.* Very good! What is something that you've learned at church or Sunday school?

Here's the next sign. *Move your hands as if you are clapping, but make no sound with them, raising them from waist to chest high.* What do you think this sign means? This sign means to praise or worship. What do we praise God for? Can you make the sign for praise without making any sound? *Lead kids in the action.*

Here's one more reason we come to church. *Hold your left hand in front of you as if you are holding an invisible glass, thumb touching fingers. With your right hand (fingers together) come up through the bottom of the glass, fingers first. As your right hand comes up through your left, open your right hand like a flower blooming.*

Can you guess what this sign means? *Let the children practice the sign and try to figure out its meaning.* This means to grow. We come to church to grow in our understanding of God. Now you try it. *Lead children in making the sign.*

Very good! Now let's put all three signs together. Follow me. We want to grow *(make the "grow" sign)* to be better friends with God. We want to be more like God by learning about him *(make the "learn" sign)* and worshiping and praising him *(make the "praise" sign).*

Great! Let's do that sentence one more time for practice, then we'll lead the congregation in doing these signs. Ready? *Lead children in the sentence using all three signs again.*

Now let's have the congregation join us. *Have children stand and face the congregation. Stand in front of the children to lead them in signing the sentence.*

Wonderful job! *Turn back to the children.* To close today, let's sign part of our prayer together. *Lead children in signing the following prayer.*

💜 Dear God, thank you for helping us learn *(sign)* about you. We praise you *(sign)* for all that you do for us. Help us to grow *(sign)* to be more like you. In Jesus' name, amen. 💜

Before you leave, I want to give each of you a paper hand. Take your paper hand home with you, and hang it somewhere where you'll see it often. Your paper hand can remind you of all the things you learn about at church. Then you can teach someone else the signs you learned here today! *Give each child a paper hand cutout.*

Happy Hand

Theme:
God has a plan for everything.

Bible Reference:
Psalm 89:11

Simple Supplies:
You'll need a Bible, a globe (you could substitute a world map), and globe stickers.

et's talk today about some of the wonderful things God has made. *Place the globe in front of you.* When God made the world *(spin the globe)*, he said that every part of it was good. Because God made our world, he understands it perfectly. He can see the whole earth. *Spin the globe again.* We can only see a small part of the world at a time. But God sees the biggest elephants and the littlest bugs, all over the world! What are some creatures that God can see right now in our world? *If the children need prompting, point to places on the globe and ask, "What can God see in the jungle?" and "What can God see in the ocean?"*

God not only sees all the creatures of the world, he has a plan for each one. What kinds of jobs did God give cows? Why do you think God make dogs? What job do you think God gave the mosquito? *Almost whatever the kids answer, you can respond with "You may be right."*

Mosquitoes are pretty pesky to us. But even mosquitoes have a place in the world God made. For one thing, they provide food for bats and birds. From the little baby mosquito to the tallest giraffe, God has a plan for every creature in the world. *Open your Bible to Psalm 89:11.* Listen to what the Bible says in Psalm 89:11. I'll read a phrase of this verse, and you repeat it back to me:

The heavens are yours *(have children repeat the phrase)*,
and yours also the earth *(repeat)*;
you founded the world *(repeat)*
and all that is in it. *(Repeat.)*

This verse reminds us that God has a plan for every single thing he made—even mosquitoes! Let's put our hands on the globe as we thank God for our wonderful world. I'll say a line and then you repeat it. Ready?

💜 Creator God *(repeat)*,
thank you for this world *(Repeat.)*
and the people we love. *(Repeat.)*
Amen. *(Repeat.)* 💜

Give each child a globe sticker. Take your globe sticker home to remind you that God has a plan for every living creature in the world.

Theme:
There's only one God.

Bible Reference:
Deuteronomy 5:7-8

Why Are There Different Religions?

Simple Supplies:

You'll need a Bible, several varieties of real flowers or leaves, an artificial flower or plant (the worse the condition, the better), and a real flower or leaf for each child.

How can you tell something real from something fake?
Show kids some real flowers or leaves, then pass the flowers around the group. These are real flowers (leaves). How do we know that they're real?

Those are good answers. This real flower smells real, and feels real, and looks real. *Hold up the fake flower.* What can you tell me about this flower? *Hold it out for everyone to smell.* Does it smell the same? Look the same? How does it compare to the real flower?

You did a good job telling the real flower from the fake one. How can you tell that God is real? *Allow children time to respond. Then open your Bible to Deuteronomy 5:7-8.*

The Bible talks about our real God, and it talks about staying away from fake gods. Listen to what the Bible says in Deuteronomy 5:7-8: "You shall have no other gods before me. You shall not make for yourself an idol in the form of anything in heaven above or on the earth beneath or in the waters below."

This verse is a command from God. God is telling us that we are not to worship anyone but God, the real, true God. What do you think that means?

There is only one God. He is the God who made the earth and everything in it. He sent his Son, Jesus, from heaven to live on earth.

There are lots of different kinds of religions in the world, just as there are lots of different kinds of people in our world. As you grow up and live for God, you'll need to be able to know which churches or religions worship the one true God and which don't.

Pick up the fake plant or flower. There are other religions that may look as if they're worshiping God, just as these fake flowers may look real at first glance. But they aren't worshiping the one, true living God at all. Some worship a person. Some worship an idol or a statue. And others worship an idea.

One good way to tell whether a church worships the one, true God is to test what they say against what the Bible says. The Bible is God's Word, and it tells us all about the one, true God.

Another good thing to do if you have questions is to talk to your parents or to other Christians. They'll be able to guide you.

But, you know, you may have some friends who go to other churches. They still worship God, but they may worship God a little differently from us. They may sing more or sing less. They may meet in a different kind of building or wear different clothes to church than we do. Those things aren't really important. The important thing is that they worship the one, true God of the Bible.

Let's go back to our flowers. *Hold up the real flowers.* How are these real flowers different from one another? *Let children answer.* That's right. These real flowers may all look a little different, but they're all still real.

Just as these flowers look different, our worship of God can look different from church to church. But we're still worshiping the one, true God.

How are these flowers alike? *Let children respond.* Right again. These flowers are alike because they're all living. The God of the Bible is alive and real, just as these flowers are alive and real.

The Bible tells us there is only one God. He's alive and he cares about us, wherever we live in the world. He listens when we pray, and he answers our prayers. He is the only real God, and the only one we should ever worship.

Give each child a real flower or leaf. Here's a reminder of what is real. Your flower is real, like the God who created it. Hold it up high as we sing "Awesome God." *Feel free to substitute any worship song the children are familiar with.*

Then close in prayer. ❤ Dear God, thank you for being the one, true God. Help us to always love and follow you. In Jesus' name, amen. ❤

Theme:
*God gave us his
Son, Jesus.*

Bible Reference:
Luke 1:31-32a; Romans 6:23b

Does God Give Us Christmas Presents?

Simple Supplies:
You'll need a Bible; the baby Jesus from a nativity scene, wrapped in a box as a present; and self-sticking bows.

What have you been doing to get ready for Christmas? How have you decorated for Christmas at your house? Have you put up your tree yet? It's an exciting time of year, isn't it?

What's the best Christmas present you've ever given someone? What's the best Christmas present you've ever received? Do you know about the Christmas present that God gave us?

I have a present here that will remind us about God's wonderful Christmas present to us. *Have a child open the wrapped box and take out the baby Jesus figure. Show the figure to all the children. Then open your Bible to Luke 1:31.*

The Bible says God sent Jesus as a gift to us. Luke 1:31-32 tells us what God's angel said to Mary when he first told her she was going to have a baby. Listen to what the Bible says: "You will be with child and give birth to a son, and you are to give him the name Jesus. He will be great and will be called the Son of the Most High."

Mary did have a baby named Jesus, and that's the very reason we celebrate Christmas every year. *Open your Bible to Romans 6:23b.* And the Bible says that Jesus is a gift from God. Listen to what the Bible says in Romans 6:23: "But the gift of God is eternal life in Christ Jesus our Lord."

Isn't that wonderful? God has given us such a precious gift in Jesus. Jesus is our way of living forever with God. That's the best gift of all! Did you ever notice that the first part of the word Christmas is Christ? That's because we're celebrating the gift of Christ!

Give each child a bow. You can put this bow on a gift you're giving to someone, or you can keep it for yourself. However you use it, let it be a reminder to you that the very best gift we'll ever get is God's gift of Jesus. Let's pray.

♥ Thank you, God, for sending Jesus as a gift to us. Thank you for letting us celebrate Jesus' birth each year with Christmas. Help us to remember that the reason for Christmas is Jesus, not the gifts we give or get. In Jesus' name, amen. ♥

Theme:
God forgives us.

Bible Reference:
Micah 7:18b

Simple Supplies:
You'll need a Bible and basketball stickers.

Do any of you like to play basketball? Who do you think is the best basketball player of all time?

I know a story about a boy named Mike who wanted to play basketball in high school. After a lot of work and practice, Mike tried out for the team. But he didn't make the team. Mike was so upset he went home and cried!

What would you do if you were Mike? Would you give up? Would you keep trying? Well, Mike did keep trying. He practiced more and more. He made mistakes, but he kept trying. And the next year, he made the team. In fact, he went on to become one of the greatest basketball players of all time. Can you guess who I'm talking about? *Allow children to guess.* Michael Jordan!

How do we learn by making mistakes? Why do we like to get a second chance after we make a mistake? When does God give us a second chance?

Every time we're sorry for something we've done wrong and we ask God to forgive us, he does. When God forgives us, he's giving us a second chance to do better, to try again. Isn't that great? God doesn't stay angry when we do wrong things. He forgives us so we can try and do the right thing the next time.

Open your Bible to Micah 7:18b. We can read in the book of Micah about God's forgiveness. Listen: "You do not stay angry forever but delight to show mercy."

What do you think mercy means? When God shows mercy, it means that God wants to show us forgiveness. God wants to give us a second chance. And then we can get better at doing what's right.

Just as Michael Jordan practiced and practiced, and is now one of the best basketball players, we can practice and become some of the best followers of God! Let's thank God for giving us a second chance!

❤ Dear God, thank you for giving us a second chance when we do wrong things. Thank you for forgiving us and letting us try again to do what is right. Amen. ❤

Give each child a basketball sticker. I have a basketball sticker for each of you to take with you. Use your sticker as a reminder that God gives us all a second chance and wants us to keep trying to do what's right!

Theme:
God sent Jesus to die for our sins, so we're forgiven.

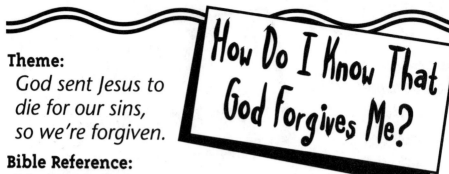

How Do I Know That God Forgives Me?

Bible Reference:
Ephesians 1:7

Simple Supplies:
You'll need a Bible and bookmarks.

Today we're going to talk a little about forgiveness. Have you ever done something that you needed to be forgiven for?

The Bible tells us that when we're sorry for something wrong we've done, we can ask God to forgive us. And when we do, God forgives us!

But some people have a hard time believing that God really forgives them. They may feel so bad about what they've done, that they can't believe that God will actually forgive them.

How can we be sure that God forgives us? To find out the answer, I have a project for you all to do. I want you to find someone in the congregation whose birthday is in the same month as yours. So if your birthday is in January, you'll need to find one person who has a birthday in January. When you find a person, ask his or her name, then come back here.

Send children out into the congregation. Encourage adults in the congregation to help children by calling out their birth months or helping the younger children on their searches. After several minutes, call all the children back, whether they've found someone or not.

Who found someone with a birthday in the same month as yours? Who did you find? *Let several children tell who they met.* How do you know the person you met has a birthday in the same month as you? *Let children answer.*

The only way you could know is because that person told you so. It's the same way with God. How do we know that God forgives us? Because the Bible tells us so! *Open your Bible to Ephesians 1:7.*

Listen while I read Ephesians 1:7: "In him we have redemption through his blood, the forgiveness of sins, in accordance with the riches of God's grace." We know that God forgives us because the Bible tells us so. God sent Jesus to die for our sins. That means we're forgiven! What wonderful news!

Give each child a bookmark. Use this bookmark in your Bible to remind you that God's forgiveness is real! Let's close with a prayer. ♥ Dear God, thank you for sending Jesus to die for our sins so we can be forgiven. In Jesus' name, amen. ♥

Theme:
God made each of us special.

Bible Reference:
Psalm 139:13-14·

Simple Supplies:
You'll need a Bible, a knife for cutting fruit, an apple corer (optional), a red apple, a green apple, and a yellow apple—enough to cut slices for everyone. If your group is large, you may want to cut some apple slices ahead of time and sprinkle them with lemon juice so they won't turn brown.

Why Did God Make People Different Colors?

L et's compare our hands today. Do you think our hands are all the same? *Let children respond.*

Let's all hold up our hands. See? We all have fingers, don't we? Now let's look more closely. Do all of our fingers look exactly alike? *Let children compare their fingers with each other and with you.*

Now choose a partner, and sit facing your partner. Besides your hands, what's another thing that you and your partner both have? It might be hair, or ears, or elbows, or even teeth! Compare those things with your partner, and see if they're exactly alike. *Give children a few moments to compare.* Well? Are your elbows all alike? How about your ears? Your feet? Is any part of you exactly like somebody else?

It's the differences between us that make each of us special. That's how God made us! Our bodies look the same in some ways and different in other ways. But we're all people who need God. And we're all people who God loves!

Hold up a yellow apple, a green apple, and a red apple in your hands. How are all these pieces of fruit alike? What's different about them?

Cut away some of the peel of each apple, and show the apples to the children. Even though they're different colors on the outside, these apples look alike on the inside, don't they? *Using either a knife or the corer/slicer, cut the apples into slices as you speak.*

Look at all the other ways these apples are alike. Each apple has a core, and seeds, and they're all about the same shape and size. God created these apples to be alike in lots of ways, but he made each one special. He just gave them each a different colored skin.

It's the same way with people. God made lots of different people. He made them alike in some ways, and different in some ways. And he made them alike on the inside, but he gave them different colored skin on the outside.

Pick up a whole apple. This is how we see each other. We see the things on the outside. *Pick up a section of apple.* This is how God sees us. He sees us inside—our thoughts and our feelings. He sees each of us as his children, no matter how we look on the outside.

Give everyone a slice of apple to eat as you continue. Then open your Bible to Psalm 139:13-14. Listen to what one man in the Bible wrote in the book of Psalms: "For you created my inmost being; you knit me together in my mother's womb. I praise you because I am fearfully and wonderfully made; your works are wonderful, I know that full well."

What are some of the wonderful things about the way God put us together? *Let children respond.* He put us together just the way he wanted. He gave us toes to wiggle. *Have children wiggle their toes.* And mouths to giggle. *Lead children in a giggle.* And he gave us hearts to love him and to love others. *Have children put their hands over their hearts.*

We are God's artwork. Just as no two apples look exactly alike, no two of us look exactly alike. But we're all alike on the inside. We all were made by God, and we're all precious to him. Let's sing a song about that.

After kids finish eating, sing "Jesus Loves the Little Children." For emphasis, when you come to the colors in the song, you can hold up a red apple and a yellow apple.

Then close in prayer. ❤ Dear God, thank you for making us. We love being your artwork. Help us to praise you for how we are made and to appreciate how you made others. Amen. ❤

If you have enough, give every child another apple slice to take as they leave.

Theme:
When we believe in Jesus, we have eternal life.

Bible Reference:
John 3:16

Simple Supplies:
You'll need a Bible, whole sunflower seeds, and a picture of a sunflower.

How many of you have ever seen a sunflower? *Show the picture of the sunflower.* Here's what a sunflower looks like. Sunflowers are very tall, with beautiful yellow flowers. But like all flowers, eventually the sunflower starts to die. By autumn, sunflowers dry up and die. What are some reasons people might be sad when the sunflowers die?

Sunflowers are a little bit like people. Have you ever known someone who has died? When that person died, how did you feel?

Just as with people, there is more to the story of the life and death of a sunflower. About the time the petals start to die on the sunflower, the center of the sunflower begins to change. *Give each child several sunflower seeds. Crack open one of the shells as you're talking.*

The center of the sunflower starts to change into seeds, just like the ones you have in your hand. Birds, squirrels, and even people love to eat these seeds. But more important, the seed can be planted. It will grow into another beautiful sunflower.

It's like that with our faith. We don't just die. We have new life inside, just like the seeds inside the sunflower shell. Our outside bodies will still die, but like the seeds inside the sunflower, we will live on. We'll live on with God in heaven if we believe in Jesus. Isn't that great to know?

Open your Bible to John 3:16. The Bible says it better than I can. Listen to John 3:16: "For God so loved the world that he gave his one and only Son, that whoever believes in him shall not perish but have eternal life."

Just as a part of the sunflower can keep living because of the seed inside, we can keep living when we believe in Jesus. We can go to live with Jesus in heaven forever when our bodies die. I'm so glad that we have Jesus!

Let's pray. ❤ Dear God, thank you for the sunflower, with its seeds that keep living. And thank you for your Son, Jesus. Because of him, we can live with you forever. Amen. ❤ *Give kids each a few more sunflowers seeds.* Take these sunflower seeds to remind you that believing in Jesus gives us new life.

Scripture Index

Theme Index